Guideposts for Leadership:
Into a New Day

Dr. C. Gail Stathis

Guideposts for Leadership:
Into a New Day
By C. Gail Stathis

EME Ministries
PO Box 73004
Ano Glyfada   16510
Greece

Copyright © C. Gail Stathis

ISBN: 1-931178-11-9

FOR ORDERING INFORMATION, PLEASE CONATCT:

VISION PUBLISHING
1115 D STREET, RAMONA CALIFORNIA
www.visionpublishingservices.com
1-800-9-VISION

DEDICATION

This has been written

... for my son, Micah, who believes in me. He always has, I see it in his eyes and know it from his smile. He never seems to doubt the leader in me.

... for my closest friend, Brian, who also believes in me. In fact, I think he sometimes believes in me more than I do. He encourages me to do more than I ever dreamed possible.

... for all my "family" at the Glyfada Christian Center and Academy. You accept me as a leader and, against all odds, you have believed in me.

And, most of all, for my God who believes in me more than anyone else, myself included.

ACKNOWLEDGMENTS

This is my very first book. I could not have written it without the help and contributions of all the people who have mentored me in leadership. It couldn't have been written without those that desired and accepted my leadership. And, of course, it definitely would not have been written without the support of my friends, who tell me I have something to say.

If one can say a leader is successful, than I can only say it is because of the many individuals who have walked alongside me and who have shared my desire to do great things in this brief time we have on earth. The following are just a few of those who have made me believe my life has counted for something:

My father, Claude, who always believed in me. Thank you!

My son, Micah, allowed me to pursue the passion of my life, even when it meant sacrificing his time with me. Thank you for reading and helping with editing of this book in a good spirit.

My friend, Brian. You were my catalyst to write this book. Your genius for words and heart of excellence continue to inspire me. Thank you for your editing and refining to make this work the best it could be.

Finally the Perfect Leader, who gifts us all with the gift of leadership. You are my passion.

Table of Contents

Introduction to the Management Series

There are many texts available regarding the topic of management and its related subjects, so as in any effort like this one, the question must be asked, why another one? What can be presented in the following pages so different from what I may find elsewhere? The answer to that question may surprise you (or not): "nothing." We are not so bold as to claim to add something *new*, but hopefully something *purposeful* nonetheless.

What do we mean by such a statement? We mean that, in this series of books, we are attempting to take principles already known and taught by many, compile them into a useful set of teachings, and use them to train and encourage us to be more diligent in our approach to life-work. Simply put, to be better at what we do. So the goal is not novelty, but relevance. We hope to be able to supply you with some of the best thoughts on the subjects involved here, and to make it interesting, provocative and effective in training.

A note about the format of the books in this series: the thoughts contained herein are garnered from a wide variety of sources. Most, if not all of them, may be attributed to an equal variety of different authors and sources. A bibliography and works cited page of many of these sources is given at the conclusion of the texts. We recognize, however, that the list may be incomplete and that some of our notes may have been developed and entered into the text without the knowledge of its point of origin. In that case, we offer our apologies to the wise originators of those thoughts, and thank them for adding quality to our work.

Books in the series include:

- *Beginning to Manage*
- *Building by Team*
- *Diverse Cultures, Diverse Leaders*
- *Guideposts for Leadership: Into a New Day*
- *Keeping Account: Basic Bookkeeping*
- *Managing Change*
- *Organizational Communication*
- *Organizing for Quality*
- *Projects and Plans*
- *Start Right, Finish Strong: A guide to coaching and mentoring*
- *The Greatest Resource: Human Resource Management*

Guideposts for Leadership:
Into a New Day

As I have reviewed many books on leadership it seems very little of what has been written on the subject has astounded the world. Though there is refinement of thought and clarity for better enabling of leaders and leadership, still many similarities exist between all the latest 'hot' books. I suggest there is "nothing new under the sun." The guidelines, traits, and characteristics for leading have been with us since the beginning of time. In fact, I believe every human has an innate ability to lead, given by their Creator.

So my reason for writing this is not about discovering new qualities or methods of leadership. It is offered more in the hope that knowledge from the classrooms of leadership training will be coupled with the day-to-day life school of leadership. I believe that would create revolutionary, excellent leaders in every area of life. My hope is that this book will trigger the universal, life-activated methods of 21st Century leadership.

In writing this book, I have thought about [my perspective of] leadership and what it is. The areas in which I have led were my starting point, and those areas where I have been a strong, courageous leader – and those areas where I

3

have failed – quickly rose to the front of my thoughts. I wondered if it has been a joy to lead and if I should really challenge everyone to find the leader inside them. My answer was an unequivocal YES!

Our understanding of leadership is not confined to corporations or committees and how they function but rather, as described in chapter one, our awareness that everyone is a leader at some time in life, in some way. To understand more clearly this idea, I had to consider that leadership is not just a position; it is a function that is often performed without the title.

A mother may give her life to lead her children because of her passion to see them be their best. A father may work non-stop hours because of passion to provide for his family in a way he was never provided for as a child. It could be said that passion is surely a factor in most leadership.

In today's world it's easy for us to just get by, showing only cursory interest in any given area. But with such an attitude life will not change, and no benefit will be realized. A true leader will not be content with this. As occasion arises, even if it costs time and personal sacrifice, a genuine concern arises in the leader to influence others for good. Barriers to that leadership will be overcome. Allow me if you will to borrow from the Bible as an example. God said to a reluctant, tongue-tied Moses, "I will help you speak and teach you what to say." (Exodus 4:12) Moses

ultimately did respond and fulfill an irreplace-
able role for his people. True leaders, reluctant
or not, want to influence for the better, for the
good.

It is fundamental to grasp that everyone has
leadership potential, but not everyone is living
up to the potential within them. It takes
courage; it costs and it's tiring, but it's also
rewarding. Is it worth it? If one were to take up
the gauntlet, to rise up to lead where innate
strengths prove ample for the task, is it really
worth it? Yes, I say, and YES again.

Discover with me, if you will, the guideposts that
will lead us into that new day. Reluctantly or
full of zeal, let us discuss at least some of what
it takes to bring the potential for leadership to
fruition in us all.

Though no one can go back and make a brand new start, anyone can start from now and make a brand new ending.
- Anonymous

It's never too late to be who you might have been.
- George Elliot

I can do everything through him who gives me strength.
- St. Paul

Chapter One
The Attitude of Leadership

It is interesting to me that modern leadership studies are turning attention these days to the fact that leadership is not simply a business concept or a set of principles to be enacted in a corporate setting. We are beginning to understand at a deeper level what many have said for a long time: the phrase "Leaders are born, not made" is a myth that hinders many potential leaders. Leadership in any public incarnation actually begins at the private level. *Leadership is first about the person, and then about the tasks that the person performs.* That is where we will begin: in the heart and mind of the would-be leader.

Consider Mr. X. Commanding and making decisions was just part of everyday work life. As one of the primary leaders of a corporation listed on a prestigious world stock exchange, Mr. X had a dignified and well earned reputation; the world did seem in fact to be his oyster. He had a beautiful wife and two wonderful children. His education was earned from among the best institutions, preparing him for a life in which his every dream became the reality. With a spotless reputation, not only at the work place but also among his peers in his social clubs, church, at the gym and the local grocer... the question was, could it get any better?

Mr. X knew he was a leader and had charted the course of his life to continually rise to the next level. A bit austere in manner, he exuded self-confidence. Never really had his decisions been challenged. Yet the day came when his confidence meandered into arenas where his leadership skills had not been challenged or tested. Mr. X, so certain of his leadership abilities, never conferred with others. He was a leader. Perhaps his attitude was that no one else had the same leadership gifting. Manipulating company funds, he would later say he was only thinking of profitability for the company. After financial disaster struck and he was questioned as to how it happened, there was no logical response. He was a leader; leaders do not need the counsel of other, lesser qualified persons.

An employee discovered it. As reports began to cross her desk, she realized something was wrong and she reported the matter to upper management. The company was saved, but not before loss of hundreds of thousands of dollars. She reported the problem because of a spirit of leadership operating in her. Leadership, you ask? Yes. We all have the ability to be leaders.

EVERY PERSON HAS LEADERSHIP POTENTIAL

You do, and this book is about you. It is about finding and knowing how you can be a leader in the 21st century.

Society has held a misconception: the person with obvious or emergent leadership skills is the only leader. Consider the possibility that this is not a truism. Rather, let it be assumed for the purposes of this study that all humans have an innate ability to lead in some area of life or work. The problem: very few people ever realize or actuate their ability to adeptly lead in the areas of possibilities.

It is often easier to be a follower than a leader. We let someone else do the work and make the decisions. Yet there is always unrest among the followers, concern that decisions made by the leaders are less than ideal. Perhaps you don't want to be a leader. I re-state however: in some time and place, in some realm of life, every human will be called to lead.

Consider a few examples of leadership[1]:

- A mother who spends time with her child
- A friend who risks alienation to confront a moral failure
- A corporate executive who rejects offers of inside information
- A husband and wife who work together on day-to-day finances
- A teacher who stirs curiosity in the minds of her students
- A military commander who orders his troops into harm's way
- A nurse who works with the anger of a stroke victim

- A missionary doctor, treating patients in spite of personal risk
- A child who speaks as advocate for his aging parents
- A terminally ill patient who demonstrates grace and courage
- A government official who takes an unpopular political stand

In the usual definitions of leadership, the above would probably not be considered examples of such, but in each situation we can see someone influencing and affecting another life. That is leadership. The premise of this book is to explore an everyday theme of *what it is to be a leader.* Certainly, an understanding first must come as to *what a leader is,* in order to understand how leadership is exhibited and operated in a person's life. It is to be hoped that understanding this fact will empower distinguished leadership which, in turn, will empower distinguished followers. Subsequently, each person is enabled to lead and follow well as the situation requires.

LEADERSHIP TRUTH:
Every person is a leader <u>and</u> a follower in some arena of his life.

Problem: Society has been weakened. Humanity stands on unsure foundations, partly, at least, because of leadership in the past that has been ineffective, prideful, fearful and indifferent to any sensible notion of leadership skill and style.

Solution: In the days ahead, a new breed of leaders must arise.

What is the way forward? The answer to that may be complex. For our purposes, however, it is first of all to find the leader in you. You must develop that potential in order to lead in the arenas of your personal influence. And then you are to birth other leaders around you; *leadership begins in you.* It is first and foremost something birthed in your attitude. That is a primary key to the facilitation of true leadership; that understanding separates the leader from the follower in any given circumstance or situation.

To define some classic characteristics of a true leader it is necessary to establish a foundational appreciation of leadership. Allow me to provide a few perspectives.

LEADERSHIP BEGINS WITH ATTITUDE

When a person's life affects or influences another, whether for the positive or negative, then leadership potentials are in action. It is time to awaken the dream in each of us. It has been said, 'You are what you believe.' What do you think your life should be?

Taking hold of and enacting those thoughts and desires; implementing a plan of action to see them empowered, makes you a leader in life. The cry for true leadership has never been louder.   This encompasses every aspect of life, whether it is the role of *leadership in life arenas* (such as your role as a parent, spouse, or friend) or in *organizational structures* such as corporations, governments, congregations, and the marketplace.

Leaders will come and go in the corporate, organizational world. But, true leaders that will make a difference in lives are those that exhibit exceptional character qualities, and utilize those qualities at all times, even in, or especially in, daily life relationships.

How then do we recognize true leaders and the areas in which each one leads or has the potential to lead? Are there areas in which you are relinquishing your leadership role out of lack of understanding that you *should* lead?   And, how does one take up the mantle that has been cast off or handed to another person who is less capable or already overburdened with trying to lead in too many areas? A cursory glance of credible, present day opinions describes the ideal leader as one who:

- Has distinct thought processes
- Possesses attitudes that are strong and confident
- Esteems others around him/her
- Has influence
- Is not a dictator
- Is a visionary, inspiring others to follow
- Is driven by passion for an embraced cause

There is a crisis in true leadership in the world today. The prevailing attitude seems to be, "Let someone else be in charge." (Or better, "Let me be in charge. Let someone else have the responsibility.") Have we come to this state of affairs because of the lack of people with leadership knowledge and skills? Is there any practical knowledge available for leading in any given situation? The world is desperate in every arena for a "how to" directive.

In a perusal of the testimonials of many leading, corporate figures, one of the single most impressive common denominators identified of great leaders is that *they do not lead double lives.* They have a passion for living that is carried out through the personal as well as corporate life. How do you live your life? The leadership skills in each person are strengths and character qualities that are lived out day by day in each and every part of life, whether in making decisions of a major caliber or simply deciding to take time for a nap so the family will not be encumbered with a grouchy leader.

So, I ask, how are we to live life differently, knowing that true leaders cannot be made into leaders but *are* leaders? Perhaps you are in a leadership role at present and think that, although you're failing miserably, you want to be the leader you know you can be. Or, perhaps, you have never thought of yourself as a leader but you have a desire to accomplish your full potential. How do you go forward from here and live differently, live as a leader? It is possible,

13

but it might require a change of attitude. Consider some of these concerns for modern leadership.

LEADERSHIP TRUTH:
Desiring to be all you can be with integrity and with passion is a key demand from this time forward!

You must recognize that desire is not enough. The world is full of people desiring more from life; desiring to be something they are not. To be a leader in the 21st century, you must take that desire and move forward. There must be an activation of thought and attitude that causes you to believe that transformation is possible and *probable.* But, as with anything of value, there is a cost. It requires you to be committed for the rest of your life to the attitudes and thought processes of a leader.

The world is controlled by the immediate moment; the media has affected our ability to be patient and wait to see change and development. If you are controlled by an attitude desiring to always see immediate results, certainly this is a good place to begin your journey toward "becoming" something else.

The need for immediate gratification leaves you a slave to the immediate circumstances. Rather than putting yourself in the position if serving the circumstances of life, begin to realize that these situations can serve you and, at the same time, improve quality of life for others.

Perhaps, for clarity's sake, it can be called a transformational pilgrimage. In the classic tale, *Pilgrim's Progress,* a personal favorite, the lead character started a journey; he was often certain throughout that he was nearing his ultimate destination. He was disappointed at various delays along the way, hindered by hardship and circumstance. To his credit, he continued and ultimately reached his destination. *The modern leader understands persistence in the journey.* He understands that the transformation will not come immediately, nor may it come easily; and he is ready for the challenge!

But the path of a leader is also not a path traveled alone. Leaders must necessarily have followers. As on any successful journey, the people traveling together cannot be going in different directions. A leader is not made by a title, and does not need one; rather a leader decides on a course and ensures that everyone is going the same direction. A leader always has someone following, because the sense of direction is felt and affirmed by those following. Genuine leadership is recognized by others, who then mirror the leader's direction and join him or her in the journey.

Beware along this way that your attitudes will be reflected in your actions. Who do you think you are? To whom are you accountable? Your answers to questions such as these come from deep inside, but the evidence of them is manifested in your actions. Regardless of the destination, your answers to these questions determine your perspective for the journey, whether as leader or as follower. Basically it works like this: if you think you are a follower in any given situation, you will be a follower. If you think you are a leader in any situation, you will strive to lead. The ultimate goal is to know where and when to follow and where and when to lead. Settling these questions will empower every individual to lead or follow with integrity and passion.

In this beginning chapter, it must be understood that whether you see yourself as a follower or leader, *no individual can please everyone.* Therefore, I return once again to the premise that your attitude must be based in the knowledge of who you are. That will give birth to and sustain the individual, whether exercising the role of a leader or follower. Once you perceive who you are and why you are here, you will then understand your significance and find your leadership roles.

Becoming a leader is all about personal trans-formation, and it most certainly isn't limited to corporate presidents. Whoever you are, it is imperative that you discover your leadership potential. It requires that you know yourself and believe that you were created to make this world a better place. Titles don't make you a leader, but attitudes that result in actions do. Leadership happens when you realize that:

- You have something within you that is enjoyable and useful and can be developed, both for your benefit and for the good of others.

- You desire to serve, not always to be served.
- You see the good in others and want to help develop it.
- You understand that there are times when the mindset to lead must be cultivated.
- You understand that there are times to be a follower.
- You do not want to be in control of everything, but neither will you be overcome by situations.
- You want to manage the environment, not control it.
- You understand that leadership demands honesty and integrity.
- You understand that a leader must think of the future.
- You choose to think about what is important and why.
- You have strong feelings about issues.

I have heard the story that, in his presentations, John Maxwell speaks of a group of children who were asked, "What is a leader?" Their resulting group definition was, "A leader is someone who knows the way, goes the way and shows the way." Surely, no one knows the direction to every place, so how can we find the right way and then, in turn, show others? It is a noble pursuit, and *when leadership is understood as a role to benefit others and not just self,* then and only then will the inherent desire to exercise leadership emerge. That desire to discover and lead.

LEADERSHIP IS NOT SYNONYMOUS WITH PUBLIC PERSONA

Leadership is every person's potential destiny, but before it can happen, one must believe! Leadership doesn't mean your name will be in lights or that you'll become famous. Leadership will be seen in the way you live; it will be evident in the real and potential impact that your attitudes and actions generate in the lives of others. Consider the questions below, attributed to Charles Schultz, creator of the comic strip "Peanuts". It's not necessary to answer the questions; the point should be clear at the end of the reading.

1. Name the five wealthiest people in the world.
2. Name the last five Heisman trophy winners.
3. Name the last five winners of the Miss America contest. (Or, any country's beauty pageant.)
4. Name ten people who have won the Nobel or Pulitzer Prize.
5. Name the last half dozen Academy Award winners for best actor and actress.

If you were to answer similarly to most of those that were questioned, not many answers would be forthcoming. The point is that making headlines does not insure lasting recognition or applause. Note: the winners were first in their appropriate areas, but trophies tarnish and awards are forgotten. Accolades and certificates are buried with their owners. It would benefit us in this study to examine leadership from another angle. See how you do on this one:

1. Name two teachers from school that impacted your life.
2. Name three friends who have helped you through a difficult time.
3. Name a few people who have taught you at least one principle in life you try to live by.
4. Think of a few people who have made you feel appreciated and special.
5. Think of five people with whom you enjoy spending time.

Certainly, most respondents were able to place names alongside at least a majority of these questions. These are the names of those who have modeled leadership in your life. Remember, *leadership is not only a role that benefits self, but it is a role that is primarily intended to benefit others.* The people who make a difference in life are not the ones with the most credentials, the most money, or the most awards. They are the ones who care. They are influencers! Leaders!

It serves the point to glance at another thought from Mark Sanborn, author of, *The Fred Factor*[2], a book written on the topic of success in business today. His number one point: Believe that everybody makes a difference. You don't need a title to be a leader and influence others. As leaders we should ask ourselves, "What invitation to greatness do we extend to others?"

The problem: most people do not think of themselves as leaders at all. But, every issue in life will encompass the need for some perspective on leadership relative to the situation. If leadership is exhibited appropriately in the home, there is success; if it is exhibited with friendships, again, there is success. The same is true for business, church, clubs and associations. When there is failure, it is often based on the failure of someone to exercise leadership attitudes and skills.

Leadership is influence: the ability to persuade and to guide, to affect a particular outcome. This implies that there is a large variety of leadership styles, from the charismatic leader of multitudes through to the relational leader, one person who influences another. Yes, each one of us has the ability to lead.

In the 21st century we must live beyond understandings and convictions of the past. We live in a new day; one that demands that we build on the lessons of the past. And then we must take them to the next level: a level of excellence. *What do you believe about yourself?* Beliefs, thought patterns and convictions construct the framework of our lives. Is your building a work-in-progress or is it condemned? Perhaps your identity resides in a turn-of-the-20th century decaying mansion, old, creaky and cold. It's time to move forward into a new development, the 21st century model!

Desiring to live to the fullest and to do it with excellence will require that your belief patterns be examined. You will be called upon to explore the leader within you. You will also be required, as any true leader is, to excel as a follower when it is time. Success will require discernment: when are you to lead? And when are you to follow?

> ### LEADERSHIP TRUTH:
> *Sometimes we enable, sometimes we are enabled. Sometimes we lead, sometimes we follow. Wisdom knows the difference, knows when and where to perform a function.*

Dr. Myles Munroe, in *The Spirit of Leadership*[3], has examined some of the myths that hinder us from living beyond the personal philosophies we have relied on in the past. Briefly they are:

- Myth One: Leaders are born, not made. This philosophy blocks our own leadership potential.

- Myth Two: Leadership by providence. Certain people are chosen by the 'gods'.

- Myth Three: Leadership is the result of a charismatic personality. This is the theory that only certain individuals possess the unique charisma necessary for leadership.

- Myth Four: Leadership is the product of a forceful personality. This false perception comes from the idea that people are fundamentally incompetent and naturally lazy and must be forced and manipulated by leaders if anything is to be accomplished.

- Myth Five: Leadership is the result of special training. Many people feel they have to have an MBA or attend leadership conferences to be able to lead others.

In the beginning of the 21st century, we live in a world where news reports tell of little boys that smash in the brains of infants; a world where madmen reign terror on innocents; a world where divorce is considered even prior to the marriage; a world where even the concept of absolute truth is considered funny, even dead. I can't help but believe that many of us have surrendered our will to someone or something else.

If you have a point of view, you have potential for leadership. If you have a perspective, whether it's different from others or the same, speaking it out exhibits leadership possibilities. Just because someone is in power, has the title of leader, does not mean they should lead our every decision, our will, our character and beliefs. We must rise to be the beautiful, powerful, vital creations we are capable of being. Philosophies are made to be queried, questioned and only adapted when proven reasonably true. Many philosophies have fallen by the wayside. Many more must fall by the wayside if we are to move into a new and better 21st century.

Outside my home there is a motorcycle. I don't ride it. Why? Years ago, I fell and seriously injured my foot. Though I have tried several times since that fall to ride it, I lost the spirit of being a motorcyclist. The courage and desire is not what it once was. Leadership is like that. Imagine that life is like that motorcycle. You were a rider before. You have led in some areas, but because of disappointments and difficulties, or because no beneficial effect was evident from all your efforts, great drive doesn't exist in your character anymore. And, so the motorcycle sits in the driveway. You have forgotten you are a motorcyclist. You forgot you are a leader.

The challenge of this book is for everyone to find a renewed understanding of purpose. Each individual was born to be a leader. So you can stop making excuses. But it's not easy. There are challenges ahead. You must be all you can be. Each person must embrace that under-standing if our world, if this 21st century, is to be renewed, energized and moved forward.

Regardless of your present circumstance, regardless of your present self image, the truth remains: each individual is a leader in some area. Believe it. You must!

We make a living by what we get.
We make a life by what we give.
- Winston Churchill

Business is at a crossroads. Capitalism
is facing a crisis. All of us who believe
in business – from CEOs to business-
school professors – must recognize that
we have contributed to this crisis.
-Fast Company "Memo to: CEOs", June, 2002

You know why the guys at the top
have such large offices? It is to house
their huge egos.
- Anonymous

Chapter Two
Transformational Leadership

A few years ago, the new director of British Airways decided one of his first actions should be to go to the airport and take a flight. The first-class area was full and the reservations staff was going to move someone out of first class in order to give him a seat. He said, "No. These are people who have paid for tickets. Give me whatever's available." But the only available seat was one in the last row, and that seat did not even recline. He took it. The former CEO of the company would never have done something like that. Later, when he was on board and seated, the flight attendant rushed back to him with magazines and said, "We've got a few magazines left." The CEO said, "Give it to the paying customers first. If there's anything left, I'll take one." Of course, there was nothing left.

Once they had landed and the word got out about these events, the story shot through the company in seconds. It was recounted over and over again around water coolers and lunch tables, for ages, as if it had happened just last week. Why? What was the intrigue? It was the message that this CEO's actions potently displayed: the customer comes first. All of the talk that is so often associated with customer service policy was at once modeled in his simple effort.[4]

It is a common understanding regarding leadership in almost any arena that we can only lead others along the path as far as we, ourselves, have traveled, or at least are willing to travel first; to merely point the way is not enough. Real leaders are said to be in short supply; at least, those who are willing to sit at the back of the airplane in order to exemplify a personal message of what the company wants to be seem to be in short supply! The search is on.

In the last twenty years, interest in studying leadership development has exploded. Items of note in the discipline of leadership studies seem to fall under two general headings: 1) The proliferation of leadership development methods; 2) The importance of a leader's emotional stability and impact on others.[5]

There was a time when classroom instruction was viewed as the epitome of the learning experience. Today, however, there is more emphasis on the value of day-to-day life experience. Training is important, but as the topic of leadership is being explored, there appears to be an undeniable value placed on our experiences at work and in life in general. In the future, leadership development methods will not be based solely on the classroom. Relationships, methods of coaching, mentoring, and the like are invaluable tools for the recognition of leadership and its development as we move into the 21st century. Life is paved with many and diverse learning environments... those in the classroom as well as those in the grocery store, and those in the work environment and around the kitchen table.

The general lack of understanding in issues of leadership and related concepts needs to be confronted. Items of concern include improving our ability to interact with the emotional needs of others, understanding the stresses of life, the shift in work ethic from one of commitment and responsibility to a focus on rights and privileges. True leadership is certainly key to social advancement. Most people lack self awareness, and that lack rebounds into society at large. The implication is that if someone is not aware of the need or opportunity to learn, they probably will not learn.

Another factor at work, in my opinion, is the increasingly pessimistic view that many people take toward genuine leadership. Perhaps in an increasingly technical world we lack the element of faith which underlies a willingness to be led. With no faith, we are less trusting and therefore less willing to believe in our leaders, and as a consequence, their leadership and our own value as followers are diminished.

So what is the point? John Maxwell, a well-known author and mentor of leaders, speaks of the notion of modeling actions before attempting to lead others in that action. As in the story of the British Airlines CEO, leading is not so much about telling as it is about doing. There is a great need, as leaders seek to impact others with emotional significance, to model an awareness of the value of leadership and enhance the view of leadership as a noble pursuit.

LEADERSHIP TRUTH:
Leadership is the key to every important advance and accomplishment in human society.

INTRODUCING EMOTIONAL INTELLIGENCE

Clinical Psychologist, Daniel Goleman, named and defined emotional intelligence in 1998, as *the capacity for recognizing our own feelings and those of others, for motivating ourselves, and for managing emotions well in our own selves and in our relationships.*[6] Although the concept had been part of leadership training for a number of years, it had never before been so clearly defined as a distinct part of leadership training.

The term 'emotional intelligence' describes abilities distinct from, but complementary to, academic intelligence; or, those purely cognitive capacities measured by IQ. The term encompasses so many additional qualities. It has become clear that leaders and managers must move beyond strictly intellectual know-how if they hope to motivate themselves and their co-workers.

How is emotional intelligence related to the specific behaviors we associate with leadership effectiveness? The Center for Creative Leadership conducted a study based on data from

28

three hundred two managers between July and September, 2000. Their documented findings indicate that higher levels of emotional intelligence are associated with better performance in the following areas[7]:

- Participative Management
- Putting People at Ease
- Self-Awareness
- Balance Between Personal Life and Work
- Straightforwardness and Composure
- Building and Mending Relationships
- Doing Whatever it Takes
- Decisiveness
- Confronting Problem Employees
- Change Management

Additionally, on-going studies revealed that key leadership skills and perspectives are actually related to aspects of emotional intelligence, and that career derailment was directly related to the absence of emotional intelligence. (The study findings may be reviewed in greater detail by visiting the website www.ccl.org.)

Conclusions: Leadership abilities vary according to their relationship to, and level of emotional intelligence. In general, co-workers seem to appreciate a manager's ability to control his impulses and anger, to withstand adverse events and stressful situations, to be relatively happy with life, and to be a cooperative member of the group. Such leaders are more likely to be seen as participative, self-aware, composed, and balanced.[8]

What can we do to improve leadership skills and perceptions of emotional intelligence? The need to increase self-awareness cannot be overstated as a key in this quest for leadership development. Being in leadership is often stressful; therefore, as self awareness is developed, it enables emotional disturbances to be more readily identified and monitored, leading to quicker recovery time when they do occur.

This is where *coaching and mentoring* become so vital. Self-awareness can best be developed through the practice of seeking on-going feedback. Those who know you well and are amenable to honest reflection can share how your behavior is impacting them and others. For example, reflect for a moment upon adversity, business failures, demotions, missed promotions, unchallenging jobs, and personal trauma. Were there lessons learned through these hardships? Self awareness studies are often part of leadership development seminars. Why? We learn from our failures as well as from our successes, and such studies help us to process those experiences and grow from them. Self-awareness can be accomplished without the time and expense of formal seminars.

For long-term career success, it is also critical to learn how to be a cooperative, contributing, and constructive member of a team. Emotional intelligence adds to one's ability to manage and lead resistant followers. It equips us to help others become valuable team contributors as we model those practices.

The gift of understanding and the appropriate application of emotional intelligence are major areas of concern that must be addressed if we are to become effective leaders. Effort must be put into it. For example, if maintaining self-control is an area of weakness for you, consider leading a project team made up of diverse members or taking calls on a customer hot line. Observe others known for their strength and integrity in managing crisis situations. Consider the potential for improvement in your leadership development; what steps could you take to enhance your strengths?

Does such emotional consideration mean a person becomes soft in order to lead? No, as one study stated, emotional intelligence is not being soft; *it is being intelligent with emotions.* It is the ability to observe, acquire and apply knowledge from the realm of emotions, while leading yourself and others. It is ineffective and im-practical to consider the emotional concerns of both the leaders and those who are led as separate or somehow irrelevant (or at least undesirable) elements of interaction. They do exist. So, how do we deal with them? Answers to that question will help us to become effective in our leadership capacities.

There are five important parts to this effort.[9]

- Know what you are feeling.
- Manage your own feelings, especially distressing ones.
- Be self-motivated.

31

- Develop and practice empathy.
- Manage relationships.

Interestingly, this is not just a new gimmick to get attention for the latest leadership book; the concept of emotional intelligence is based on brain research. Research shows that these skills are different from technical and purely cognitive abilities because they involve a different part of the brain — the emotional center rather than the neocortex, which is the center of senses, logical thought, language, etc. For a long time, leadership has dwelt on the cognitive, without considering the emotional. The 21st century leader will learn to take both into account.

Evidence supporting the critical importance of emotional intelligence is mounting. Goleman, in his landmark Harvard Business Review article, *"What Makes a Leader,"*[10] shares insight into the power of emotional intelligence:

> "...when I calculated the ratio of technical skills, IQ and emotional intelligence (identified in competency models from 188 companies) as ingredients of excellent performance, emotional intelligence was twice as important as the others for jobs at all levels. Moreover, my analysis showed that emotional intelligence played an increasingly important role at the highest levels of the company, where differences in technical skills are of negligible importance. In short, the

numbers are beginning to tell us a persuasive story about the link between a company's success and the emotional intelligence of its leaders. And just as importantly, research is also demonstrating that people can, if they take the right approach, develop their emotional intelligence."

As research and study continues into this area, it is being further discovered that developing emotional intelligence skills not only benefits the bottom line for corporations, but builds the individual as well. It is the win/win scenario of organizational development. Byron Stock & Associates, a leading group in the exploration of emotional intelligence, has shared some important in-sights as they have studied it.

"Our perceptions become the lens through which we see, process, and interpret events. Our perceptions to events around us trigger our thoughts and emotions. It is not the event that drives our behavior, but rather, our perception of that event. Once we choose a perception (or interpretation) of the event, it immediately triggers thoughts and emotions. These thoughts and especially feelings can generate profound and instantaneous electrical changes in the heart and Autonomic Nervous System (ANS) which have effects throughout the entire body and brain."[11]

"The nervous system (ANS) causes biochemical changes which have powerful affects on our bodies and our ability to think. The consequences (effects) of our perceptions profoundly affect our ...

- Physical Energy - (rate of aging, stamina and endurance, hormonal balance, immune function)
- Mental Clarity - (ability to con-centrate, decision-making Skills, problem-solving ability, clarity of per-ception)
- Emotional Balance - (stability, level of reactivity, responsibility and maturity, level of fulfillment)
- Personal Effectiveness - (self em-powerment, communication skills, creativity, intuitive awareness)"[12]

According to the myriad groups and institutes now researching this area of leadership devel-opment, there is good news: emotional intel-ligence skills can be learned. However, there is a caution, because typical training methods will not work. This is because the emotional center of the brain learns best through motivation, extended practice, and feedback. In order to develop emotional intelligence skills, old behaviors must be eliminated and replaced with new ones. Most of us have learned by now that this is asking a lot. It cannot happen, of course, in a weekend seminar, or in the time typically allocated for training in most settings.

It would appear from these illuminating studies that, if the approach to leadership training into this 21st century will incorporate time to reinforce the skills introduced, a way to motivate their application on a regular basis, and re-enforcement of positive behavior, leaders will ultimately manifest emotional intelligence *coupled with* I.Q. and technical skills. This will result in positive impacts upon organizations, business environments, the family and the individual. The bottom line: greater success.

1. Do unto others ...

2. Self Control

3. Rom, The old has gone away the new he...

Ref. Human beings are tripartite being. Sp. Sou Body
It is necess. that God should be the Lord of our whole
being, in order for us to function according to
his will.

Q.
1. ~~How~~ Can we ~~stop allowing~~ school...
negatively as such ~~portraying~~ depriving us from
doing God's will?

● Can we ~~destinguish between God's~~ the idea
we have for our self be know God or the ~~Grey~~?

3. How can we train ~~really~~ into ~~think~~ seeing ourself
God's way.

4. Is it possible for the leader to show the
way by doing or by telling?

35

To do great things is difficult; but to command great things is more difficult.
- *Friedrich Nietzsche*

A leader is one who knows the way, goes the way, and shows the way.
- *John C. Maxwell*

We never know how far reaching something we think, say or do today will affect the lives of millions tomorrow.
- *B.J. Palmer*

Chapter Three
Leaders and Leadership:
Core Definitions

The definitions of leaders and leadership twenty five years ago centered around the concepts of *obligations* and *responsibilities*. In past eras, leaders won wars, and led families and multi-national corporations, with an authoritarian style. Leadership was always envisioned from the top down. Today, it is frankly an obsolete style of leadership; times have changed. Anywhere people work, live or play together, a different mindset dominates the scene. Today, it is about *rights* and *privileges*. To be in leadership heading into the 21st century requires flexibility, and the ability to discern and to continually learn. Is it any wonder there is a shortage of leaders today?

Jim Collins is an experienced rock climber who started scaling mountains when he was a teenager. In the book, *Upward Bound: Nine Original Accounts of How Business Leaders Reached Their Summits*, Collins suggests that if failure is imminent when seeking to achieve a goal, focus should be on *'failure'* rather than failure. It derives, apparently, from a rock climbing term. When rock climbers know they cannot finish the climb, they allow themselves to fall. The ropes holding the climber are threaded through bolts attached to the rock face, and these ropes break the fall. *'Failure'*, and the willingness to experience it, indicates the commitment to go the distance, regardless of the ultimate outcome. Certainly, there are falls along the way; it comes with the sport. When the results and achievements of commitment to the sport are measured against difficulties, rock climbers believe that an occasional fall is worth the risk.

The suggestion by Jim Collins is to *commit to the summit*. Go for it aggressively and push to go as high as you can. If you fall, that's okay; it's not failure, just a detour. Leaders must commit to the responsibilities and obligations of leadership as always. However, we face changing attitudes regarding the concepts of commitment vs. rights and privileges. It's possible that you might not reach the summit. You may fall. In rock climbing, as in business, you must dare to commit to the challenge even if there are risks ahead. The 'risky path' is most frequently going to be the path forward in the 21st century.[13]

LEADERSHIP TRUTH:
Leadership is a commitment made,
in spite of risks.

So what does it take to be effective in leadership today? Why is a person chosen to lead? Are there certain characteristics, skills, abilities, and personality traits that cause some people to be chosen for leadership over others? A definition of leadership will help to address the question.

A DEFINITION OF LEADERSHIP

Leadership is about influence, guidance and direction. It is first about influencing people. The influence of leadership changes the world. Leadership enables more to be accomplished through others than could ever be done singularly. So, the role of a leader and the concerns of leadership are not about one individual; they are about people and groups of people. Leadership enables groups of people to do things they would never normally attempt alone. Therefore, leadership is an exciting group journey with joys and challenges, failures and successes!

LEADERSHIP TRUTH:
Leadership is primarily a process
of influence.

Leadership influence is the ability to persuade and to guide, to affect a particular outcome. This is a broad definition, and implies that there is a large variety of leadership styles - from that of the charismatic leader of multitudes to the relational leader, wherein one person influences another. When people do not realize their leadership *potential*, leadership *influence* lies dormant.

Leadership is also influence through relationship. Influence may be defined as an individual's affect on the thoughts and behaviors of others. In one way or another, everyone has influence. When two or more people are in relationship, they influence one other. Leaders in the 21st century and beyond will be required to exercise effective influence.

Often I hear people say they wish they had influence in a given situation or with a certain person. What many do not recognize is that their very being has an influence on others, and the world around them. Influence is defined as "having an impact on the thoughts or behaviors of others". It should be understood that words, actions, and even refusal to take part in certain activities, these all have an impact on others' thoughts and behaviors. The real question is not, 'Can I have an influence on the world?' It is, 'What kind of an influence do I choose to have?'

The next step is to recognize that tapping into resources such as knowledge, connections, positional authority, nearness to an issue... all of these contribute to how one is perceived, and they impact levels of influence.

Remember, leadership is not a new phenomenon. Early Egyptian hieroglyphics dated about 5,000 years ago display symbols for "leader." Histories of ancient cultures are replete with names and graphic descriptions of the leaders within that society. It's the same today. Every area of society - sports, education, politics, religion, and the military - develops its own icons of leadership. Their names are emblazoned on our billboards, newspapers, television and on the internet. They are our role models and they

40

reflect on and influence our values as they lead us.

Though leadership has been a topic for historians, philosophers and sociologists for thousands of years, it's only since the beginning of the twentieth century, really, that it has been studied academically. Since those studies began, over 350 known definitions of leadership have been considered and observed, yet it seems there is still confusion. For the sake of brevity and sanity, all 350 definitions will not be listed here. But for this study, it will be defined simply as follows: *A leader is a person who helps people to move from where they are presently to somewhere else* -- hopefully, to someplace better than where they were previously!

> ## LEADERSHIP TRUTH:
> ### A leader is someone who helps another to move from where he is now to somewhere else.

Based on this simple definition, it is understandable why so many people are not really progressing in their lives. So many of us today exist in survival or maintenance mode because the leadership around us is not rising to meet the need for guidance and direction. There is no place to go, and no one to help get us there. Without a leadership that emerges and actually leads, business, family, organizations, churches, just stagnate. Lack of leadership hinders the fulfillment of enriching purpose in peoples' lives.

Note in this definition that, a leader 'helps' people move. He does not make them move. The leader is out front, calling, 'this is the way, let's go.' But, he is also in the rear, picking people up when they fall and encouraging them on with a 'you can do it!' The ideal leader is also beside, 'walking with' and showing the way forward to a destination.

LEADERSHIP TRUTH:
Without leaders, people tend to stay in the same place.

Approaching leadership from the perspective of people, rather than corporations or organizations, a leader sees where people are in the present. It recognizes need for change, purposeful change -- not just change-for-change's-sake. In serving the people's needs, circumstances, and aspirations, leadership will focus on those being led. As their needs are met, the people will follow. Keep in mind, too, that this becomes a mutually dependant relationship: without followers there is no leader, without leadership there is no movement toward needs being met.

AN EXPANDED VIEW OF LEADERSHIP

While leadership is a necessary component for the advancement of society, it remains impossible to prescribe any single format or style for leaders. And, while there is no 'three-step method' to foolproof leadership, there are some foundational skills and attitudes that certainly lend themselves to more effective leadership.

Leadership involves change, so there must be movement. When leadership is effective, it will provide vision not only of *where* to go, but of *how* to go. With our definition in mind, let us expand that thought by looking at some simple statements about *effective* leadership, which as you will see tend to focus more on attitude and character than on basic skills and abilities. The reason for this is clear as you read the first item and move on from there.

- Leadership is relational; it involves people.
- Leadership is influential; people can be influenced to move toward change.
- Leadership is visionary; the leader sees where to go.
- Leadership is transformational.
- Leadership is empowerment; empowering people to take responsibility and ownership for the move.
- Leadership is personal responsibility.
- Leadership is decision-making.
- Leadership is team-building.
- Leadership is change or, rather, managing change.
- Leadership is culture, and its development.
- Leadership is communication.
- Leadership is motivation.
- Leadership is persuasion.
- Leadership is creativity.
- Leadership is self management.

- Leadership is character, or integrity.
- Leadership is credibility.
- Leadership is trust.
- Leadership is modeling.
- Leadership is servant-hood.

And the list could continue on. What might you include in the definition of a leader that is not here? When describing what a leader is, consideration must be given to what a person has to *be and do* in order to be an effective leader.

Some of the qualities coupled with the definition above might be:

- Long term effectiveness. Over time and distance, there is evidence of success.
- Ego is surrendered to humility.
- There is accessibility.
- Devotion to spouse and family is evident.
- Excellence in work.
- Character is displayed as a standard or example.

LEADERSHIP TRUTH:
Leaders are not perfect.
Some are reluctant to lead,
but they engage the task nonetheless.

History records the names of so many leaders: Martin Luther, Mother Teresa, Abraham Lincoln, Winston Churchill, Indira Gandhi, and D.L. Moody, to name a few. Looking back in your life, consider those men and women who inspired and challenged you to rise above your own limitations, to be more and to do more than you thought possible.

A group of leaders met in 1998, at a "Summit on Leadership Training" hosted by CB International, a non-governmental group. Throughout the discussions two concerns emerged: 1) "Tell us what a leader is supposed to look like," and 2) "Equip us to be that kind of leader." Becoming an effective leader does not happen overnight; it's a process. And it absolutely continues to be a work in progress, especially in these technologically advancing times.

As you read this, perhaps you are struggling with the question, "Am I really a leader, or not?" Many leaders struggle with that question. The concept that 'true leadership is comprised of unwavering confidence' is a major misperception. Leadership is found in addressing the question, not in the absence of questioning.

The call to leadership is one of life's most challenging and rewarding pursuits. Leadership authors and consultants, James Kouzes and Barry Posner state that, "Leaders are pioneers. People who take the lead are the foot soldiers in the campaigns for change." And "The unique reason for having leaders – their differentiating function – is to move us forward. Leaders get us going someplace."

If it is your personal desire to "go someplace," and it lies within your abilities to help motivate

45

Leaders and Leadership: Core Definitions

others to go along with you for their own benefit, then you, my friend, are true leadership material.

God's plan for all mankind is to lead + rule the universe He created. The Bible leaves no room for doubts that God's desire is for us to lead, He has given us the task and the potential. (Genesis)

1. If God's desire is for all mankind to lead, ~~this is why is there the need for motivation even among the~~ do we need motivation for doing so?

2. Leaders have not an easy task, ~~so being reluctant to lead~~ When leaders do not perform their job, is God's work suffering?

3. Is God going to wait on a particular person, who is delaying to accept the call?

(vv. if you don't worship, the stones will).

46

Leadership and Management are different concepts. Leadership is needed to create change. Management is needed to create orderly results.
--Anonymous

Leadership is becoming your true self for the benefit of others.
- Myles Munroe

Chapter Four
Leaders and Life-Learning

It takes real courage to be an authentic leader; because, it takes the giving of self. The work and the lifestyle demand it. You won't hear a leader say he has nothing to do, for no matter the size of the group or the varying levels of development within the group, the leader is always balancing the work to lead skillfully, while not being pulled into the details of designated work. This is a process that requires the potential leader to engage certain critical concerns.

LEADERSHIP BALANCES WORK AND LIFE

What such a person illustrates through life passions, beliefs and convictions will draw or repel followers. A leader must have courage to discover those beliefs, live by them and defend them. What an individual sees as purposeful will develop thinking patterns, pursuits and ultimately attitudes that are modeled in every facet of life. They formulate the life picture.

When personal purpose is discovered it generates passion and conviction in others. Myles Munroe has stated, "Leadership is not a pursuit but a result."[14] When individual experiences are coupled with personality strengths and character, a balance comes between the heart for the task and the skill to do the task.

These two elements—the task and the person— are two of the most crucial elements to address in order to lead effectively. They must be balanced in the life of a leader. When other people who look to this leadership are about to give up, become desperate, or don't know the way to go, the courageous leader comes to salvage the day. This service can only be offered if and because the perspectives are balanced in the leader's own experience.

Leadership can be immensely rewarding. It has incredible potential to influence for good, and good leadership generally accomplishes great things. But how is it done? Again, I do not believe there are any new revolutionary methods to be unveiled here. Perhaps, it is more just this understanding that leadership is the skill for balancing the right things in life. It is not necessarily the right personality, nor is it some ethereal, specially designated leadership gift. It has already been stated that everyone has leadership potential. But it is hard work and possesses a strong call to commitment; and there are times when leaders, just like everyone else, experience quitting urges. Finding the balance will help put a person on solid footing to keep trying and, more, striving for success.

Yes! I do believe the world, in almost every arena, is looking for those who would ride in on the white horse to save the day. It is our natural tendency to look for the "great ones" to appear. However, even after the rider makes the rescue, the task continues. Leadership requires, mandates, learning how to balance the multitude of responsibilities, personalities, processes, etc., that are its challenges.

LEADERSHIP TRUTH:
The task and the person are two crucial, conjoined elements of effective leadership.

Leadership might be described as 'messy', for the job is never fully under your control. On any given morning, a father can wake up to find his children fighting; the corporate executive can walk into the office to be hit broadside with a financial crisis; an attack of criticism can arise and therefore need to be addressed; an angry employee may suddenly resign; an important project may go haywire overnight – and the list goes on and on.

It is essential, therefore, that every leader possess and embrace his/her 'center'. Leaders are not isolated from a world that is becoming 'messier', so there must be a prioritized standard on which the skillful leader can focus in order to stay balanced, to keep from becoming lost in the myriad of difficulties and distractions.

Leading into the future requires deposits in the inner being of a leader greater than ever before. These deposits are no longer just technical skills but, as mentioned previously, include emotional intelligence and a countless collection of other intangible valuables which can only be partially touched upon in this book. These are most needed to meet the challenges of leadership in the 21st century. And it gravitates around the reality of knowing yourself, whatever the tasks or challenges; possessing an internal attitude that says, 'Yes, we can do it.' So what are some ways to develop such an individual with such qualities: such a leader? We will begin with the person who stays grounded to his center and looks to express those core qualities to others.

LEADERSHIP DEVELOPS ITSELF AND OTHERS

Organizations today recognize the value of *mentoring*, and they look for ways to formalize these types of relationships as part of their leadership development efforts. When utilized, mentoring enables what is sometimes termed action learning. A person learns by doing, and then not only is the individual transformed, but so too those who witness the transformation. Transformation is in fact contagious – to people and even to organizations.

Throughout life every person will enter into relationships that combine with experience to form the bedrock identity of who that person is. These intertwine to affect the tasks performed, the way that they are performed, and the person him or herself. Relationships that are useful for growing individual identity in terms of leadership skills and character will probably fit into one of two general groupings: *coaching* and *mentoring*. Coaching, for leadership purposes, could be defined in practical terms: a goal-focused form of one-on-one instruction and learning that ideally leads to behavioral change. Mentoring is typically defined, on the other hand, as a committed, longer-term relationship in which a senior person supports the personal and professional development of a junior person. Both are essential tools for reaching the ultimate goals.

This is because leadership that transforms must be more than a managing pursuit. We have mentioned before that leaders must often manage, but not all managers are leaders. To develop beyond management only duties, coaching and/or mentoring are the next steps for progress. Management skills could historically be defined in clear lists, sometimes functioning with no real necessary passion or purpose. [i.e. Old style management. For a discussion on the changes and modern challenges of management, see the companion book, *Beginning to Manage*, from Vision Publishing] Parents and children present a vivid picture of this principle. When lists and rules are the only means of direction, the child will rebel, be impassive or merely obey out of duty. Nothing is modeled this way, and nothing truly long-lasting is built into the learner/child. On the other hand, when the parent, as a key person in the child's life, *models* desired learning goals through their own actions, display of passion and ongoing one-on-

one interaction, the result is the ability of the parent/leader to shape the life of the child. The parent, therefore, becomes a mentor to the child.

Just like a parent, a leader has the ultimate goal of developing or changing the follower's values and sense of purpose: to lead in a way that ensures both vision and goals are accomplished. (Refer to chapter six.) On our judgments and choices will hang much of the shaping of our own lives.

A good leader will lead others beyond the attitude of clinging to 'my rights' in order to attain higher levels of commitment. Decisions will become qualifiers for the task engaged and for personal development, rather than remaining low-impact and mechanical. The goal of effecting change is inspired through the modeling of the leader, which evokes a mentoring relationship. Mentoring relationships accomplish action-oriented learning, and action through learning.

LEADERSHIP TRANSFORMS

J. A. Conger, noted author and researcher in the field of leadership studies, reviewed 15 years of transformational leadership studies conducted prior to the year 2000. At that time, the business environment worldwide was in a state of great change and pressures were increasing for companies to reinvent themselves in an ever-increasingly competitive world. Challenges to employee commitment were also at a sharp rise.

> "Prior to that time, leadership researchers generally had not distinguished between the role characteristics of leading and managing: A person in any position of authority was largely assumed to hold a leadership role. It was a novel idea that leadership and management might represent different kinds of roles and behaviors."[15]

Leadership need not be characterized by *boring work, inconsequential questions, and static answers*. Leaders are real people with real lives. Leaders influence others. At the core of the leader should exist an ability to model fundamental beliefs that, in turn, make themselves evident in an 'emotional' impact on the follower. That is, they want to follow the example. (Reflect back to chapter two.) Although the modern task of management may indeed require the character traits of leadership, some of the fundamental traits for the two enterprises differ.

In the past decade, interest has grown in topics like genuineness, authenticity, credibility, and trustworthiness in the leader. Leaders must model these values and influence those who follow. These traits are perhaps more evident through the relationships evidenced in the life of a leader than in a simple discussion of abilities.

Today's leader, with a concern for leading into the days ahead, will strive to close the gap between leader and follower. It cannot be done by simple management systems, but requires modeling through action. The leader is accessible to and aware of followers, aware of their perceptions. The influence of follower perception is paramount in effecting the process of leadership. For example, it is said that Andrew Grove, chief executive officer of Intel, works in an eight-by nine-foot cubicle in his corporate headquarters in Silicon Valley, California. He's not in a closed–off, mahogany executive suite. It may not be conducive to all work situations, but it is an illustration of reflection and effective implementation of a workable model pertinent to that situation. Leaders should seek ways of their own to accomplish the goal of accessibility and transparency.

LEADERSHIP TRUTH:
Leaders have visible lives.

In the past the objective was to train leaders to be good managers. However, in light of the changing work place, family and relationship dynamics world wide, we contend that management-only models will not work effectively in the 21st century. Whether in corporate setting or community, the home or the church, the cry is for leadership that is competent and complete. Life is the classroom. What happens at the work place, within the organization, among friends or family: these are the building blocks of our lives. Understanding that these building blocks interact and impact one another is critical. Leadership development that models the balance between work and life is essential. It opens the door to utilizing all of these building blocks and incorporating into personal, as well as corporate, development plans.

LEADERSHIP INSPIRES

In the work force today, leadership ultimately involves action, not knowledge alone. This is a critical difference between the historical characterizations of managers and leaders. Leaders combine the function of work and experience in order to gain personal knowledge and to create learning situations. Changing dynamics in worldwide employment trends illustrate that people no longer invest their entire working career in one company or corporation. Even in those organizations where service is cause-oriented and designed to enhance feelings of personal worthiness, movement from one group to another is the norm. People must be provided opportunities to learn from their work rather than being removed from their work environment in order to learn. Life is an accumulation of experiences, and these experiences provide a classroom for constant learning. It is critical that we view effective leadership models through the filters, and the resulting impact, of our life experience. Simple managers may not seek to inspire with life experiences, but leadership does.

Without leadership that inspires, the job doesn't get done as desired. Therefore, it is leaders, not traditional managers that largely sought after. For organizations of every size, the concerns of modeling leadership are becoming central to their way of life. Increasingly, organizations seek leaders who model leadership development through a strong commitment to coaching or mentoring, thereby developing their leadership base internally.

For example, at a small English-based school in Europe, staffing has always presented a substantial problem. Older, standard methods and practices called for research and advertisement in order to hire a teacher from an English speaking country. The prospective employee would come with knowledge and skills and, all being well, the employee would adapt and integrate into the new work and cultural environment. The method has not proven effective in the long term, however, as those willing to relocate are numbering fewer and fewer. Furthermore, the adjustment to a foreign culture has often failed, leaving the school in a constant state of crisis.

Consequently, in recent years the school superintendent has chosen instead, through a commitment to authentic life learning, to model leadership to a few select individuals on staff. As modeling is displayed through daily interactions, a group of aspiring educators has arisen from the ranks of volun-teers in the school. For these, training and development is accomplished in the classrooms of day to day school activity and life in general. They have not moved away to study, but are rather preparing in an environment where they can continue to interact with a leader who is actually modeling leadership, and through that interaction personally investing into the lives of those in development.

> ### *LEADERSHIP TRUTH:*
> ### *Life is an accumulation of constant experiences that provide a classroom for constant learning.*

There are many examples these days of corporations and companies that no longer train only the isolated few, 'anointed' ones identified by business college hierarchies as leaders of the future. Leadership programs and seminars are available to work groups and individuals at every level of development. Mentoring and coaching enable and equip leaders to step up to leadership needs from within the day-to-day environment. This pattern resonates emotionally with others, and such leaders become a better reflection of effective executive leadership than those who just happen to carry earned credentials.

Effective leadership is clearly about more, too, than just enacting the 'right' behaviors. It's also about reflecting attitudes and behaviors for the purpose of development. As a person's self awareness is increased it can positively impact the individual's effectiveness in relationship with others. Much leadership development feedback naturally affects how people think about themselves, not just their interactions with others. Similarly, it can lead to re-evaluations of many aspects of one's life, not just one's role as a leader. It can affect the whole person. In these ways leadership development involves the development of the whole person. The 21st century leader is dedicated to self-enhancement and is a learner engaging in ongoing *self-directed change and growth.* It follows that this process will provide a better leader or employee/follower.

Therefore, it should be assumed that leadership development includes activities to increase self-awareness and address balance in life, including the relationship between health, fitness, and leadership. Historically the description of a manager does not often include these goals; they are, however, integral to the description of a leader.

LEADERSHIP ENGAGES LIFE-LONG LEARNING

The balancing act that we have been describing throughout this chapter is an aspiration for leaders and followers, not necessarily a present reality. But with more importance being placed on leadership development in the marketplace than ever before, the sole focus is not just to develop "more and better" leaders. Although that does remain a critical goal, leadership is increasingly defined more broadly, not as what the leader does but rather as a process that brings about and is the result of *relationships.*

In this way, focus is placed on the interactions of leaders and coworkers, not just upon the so-called competencies of leadership.

Fundamentally, in making leadership development more complete, one must make sure it involves more than training. Ever more broadly, the 21st century leader impacts and directs coworkers by example. Followers see and sense this dynamic. Direction will be sought out from this type of leader more often, and in opposition to the simple management processes of a person who is only approachable when a problem arises. The dynamic is an array of developmental experiences that will meaningfully combine with each other. It would follow that leadership training never ends, for development efforts and initiatives are, and will be ongoing. Single programs or events will not suffice. People are seeking leaders that model how to live life in whatever arena they find themselves, work or play.

LEADERSHIP TRUTH:
Leadership is a living process, not a list to be completed.

Reflecting on leadership and its development, we can see the field is moving away from viewing credentials solely in terms of attributes, skills, and traits. Fine-tuning leadership competencies remains a core dimension of the activities dedicated to development in most organizations, but repeated day studies have been conducted to illustrate that leading-edge companies define

61

leadership in a more holistic manner. Today it is about skills and abilities, yes, but also about those sets of processes that guide leadership development at all levels.[16]

LEADERSHIP GAINS FROM LIFE EXPERIENCE

Historically, leadership studies have identified, or attempted to identify, a set of competencies; that is, they have tried to define the characteristics and qualities typical to success-ful leaders. Of course, effective leaders are usually characterized by certain qualities or competencies, but only developing those core qualities is not enough. How, then, are leadership capabilities most effectively engaged in development? It would seem that leadership qualities must correspond to the organization's particular identity. Company after company, the marketplace is realizing that leadership develop-ment programs implemented in isolation from the immediate business environment and it nuances rarely bring about good, long-lasting changes. It is true, therefore, that organizations must develop leaders and skill sets that correspond with and are specific to their distinct challenges and goals. Organizations with the more excellent development processes are realizing that leaders are not all the same; that further, they possess different or individual capabilities that help to make the organization successful. These companies address individual components (that is, the leaders) in ways that fit into their corporate whole. If this is the emerging pattern for leadership development, it can only be concluded that leaders should not be held accountable for demonstrating a particular set of arbitrary behaviors, but rather should be held accountable to desired outcomes.

This perspective looks beyond abilities, which have a tendency to focus on how a problem can be fixed, and instead focuses attention on the whole person, and especially the process of building on peoples' strengths and natural talents. Leaders will not be sought just because they fulfill a list of qualifications from business school; they will be sought because they exhibit strength and model great life skills in the work place.

Personal development is increasingly viewed as a process of encouraging and balancing strengths, and conversely, understanding and minimizing the impact of weaknesses. Is this not how each person endeavors to approach life successfully? The dynamics of the process might entail considering how to take action, developing learning techniques from every area of life, and transferring the wealth of that knowledge to work roles.

Helen Keller was an incredible example of the principle of taking action in her circumstances. The woman was deaf, blind, and thought to be mute. Through the miraculous intervention of, and interaction with a coach and mentor, and with Helen's decision to not settle for the 'less' of

63

her circumstance, her glaring weaknesses were minimized and she determined to live her life to the fullest. Although she was never able to see or hear, she overcame the package of difficulties and was able to effectively speak. She developed her skills and became an inspirational force and motivating *speaker* for crowds around the world.

LEADERSHIP TRUTH:
Leadership possesses the willingness to acknowledge its own weaknesses honestly.

Someone once said, "Leadership is 95 percent perspiration and 5 percent inspiration." It is not enough to *know* strengths and weakness; action must be taken to address them. Placing ones feet into the shoes of leadership is a big job. Life can be confusing, sometimes priorities are too. What better classroom could there be than life experiences? Incorporate them into your overall action plan of leadership development.

Since the path to learning weaves its way all through life, it simply makes sense to apply this kind of learning to leadership development. In the work environment, it has been believed that learning emanates from classroom and training experiences, mentoring experiences, and challenging assignments. But there is another source—personal life experiences! In the past it was thought that these actually just conflicted with work, causing stress and exhaustion and pressure. The truth of that cannot be denied; however, personal life experiences can also offer rich career benefits because of the perspective they provide and the opportunity to learn valuable skills.

One survey was conducted asking employees about off-the-job experiences and how they were perceived to develop leadership skills and perspectives. A sampling of the responses follows. Respondents actually identified certain life experiences that helped them to perform effectively on the job[17]:

1. ***Opportunities to enrich interpersonal skills.*** Interpersonal skills are developed because parents, spouses, in-laws, step-parents, friends, and community volunteers are directly relevant to the collaborative, conflict management, and influencing skills so needed in business.

2. ***Psychological benefits.*** Having a rich personal life helps you view your work more objectively and to keep things in perspective. In addition, feelings of self-esteem derived from personal activities contribute to the sense of confidence necessary for handling challenges at work. During times of challenge and crisis, it is helpful to have positive experiences away from work.

3. ***Emotional support and advice.*** Family and friends can act as sounding boards and motivators, providing advice and insights that help in difficult work situations. A strong support network can help you figure

out what risks to take, how to leverage strengths, and how to shore up weakness. Offerings of differing and varying perspectives can broaden the thinking process.

4. ***Learning to handle multiple tasks.***
   Juggling multiple tasks and responsibilities at home can be good practice for doing so at work—promoting efficiency.

This process of drawing on life experiences to add benefit to the work environment is, in reality, already present. Whether or not we recognize it, and regardless of how formally we approach it, it exists. Our persona outside of the office affects who we are inside the office, both for the positive and the negative. Acknowledgement of this fact– and addressing the positive and negative qualities that derive from it– will bring us the benefit of learning. That being said, it is important to take note that, while life informs work and work informs life, they are not fundamentally the same thing.

LEADERSHIP DISCERNS THE WORK/LIFE RELATIONSHIP

If the identity of a leader in the 21st century will be so closely reflected in work, and that has been the case for quite awhile, then work must be kept in balance with home and off-the-job experience. *A leader is not the work.* I suggest that the leader with the greatest future impact will understand the dynamics of a world where work is necessary. But the entire life can and must be incorporated to reflect an emotional, living being in possession of other practical activities. There will be participation in the world, not just in work. Life at work must be shaped by the people, rather than work shaping an entire life. Yes, work sustains and develops towns, homes, schools, communications, etc., but as the dynamics of this prominent part of life become more complex and intensive, care must be taken to not become a slave to the mechanics.

LEADERSHIP TRUTH:
For balance, remember a leader is
not the work. That's slavery.

It cannot be re-stated enough: as never before, life is one of constant change. Leaders face unrelenting competition in the work place. Managing stress and personal renewal is the goal for work as well as home. Much has been written about how to avoid burn-out. Dealing with multiple and competing demands of a fast-paced career and personal/family relationships and responsibilities is difficult.

It is a common challenge though, and there is increasing recognition that a person's work and personal life have reciprocal effects on each other. Studies have concluded that individual leader effectiveness is enhanced when multiple roles are managed at home and at work. This, of course, equally applies to employees or members of any group. More is being done to learn about the benefits to organizations and even the benefits to family and community in this interaction.

As studies continue to look at the effect of work and personal life, personal effectiveness as a leader is definitely associated with better health and exercise.[18] Moving into the future, it is imperative to better understand ideas about organizational life that are challenged by work and life integration. With modern day pressures and stresses mounting, organizations will need to make changes to facilitate greater work and life integration. The lines are very often blurred and becoming more so.

LEADERSHIP TRUTH:
Resilience is non-negotiable for leadership in the 21st century.

How will a leader balance work and life? Resilience is the beginning of the answer. It is a non-negotiable commodity necessary for leadership. Work and life situations will always bring challenges that become integrally related. Resilience is the ability to bounce back from adversity or hardship. An attitude and practice of resilience develops a characteristic that will become obvious as it is continually developed in a person's life. We must deal with hardships in a manner that displays personal growth, and develop the ability to cope with (and successfully pass through) difficulty. One of the fundamental characteristics of resilience is that it allows difficult experiences in life to be useful as opportunities to learn. Such experience equips us to confront hardship successfully as time passes.

The 21st century leader, whether man or woman, will want to *celebrate* life, not *endure* it. A leader that can model how to maneuver through the radical discontinuity of day-to-day life wherever it is lived—home, work, with friends— has the potential to transform the environment and time. Leaders will set the tone for life around them, and resilience is a necessary component. Everything must be viewed appropriately, as through a lens that sets the situation in its proper perspective. What is worth tackling, what should be cast off? What is excess? Practices of excess cannot rule the day. To coin a familiar phrase, time is of the essence. Time is a critical value in every circumstance. The person who can identify those things that waste time, emotion, or involvement, and then work through those issues to a more effective use of time and energy, will certainly be desired as, and probably designated a leader.[19]

LEADERSHIP FOLLOWS THE GUIDEPOSTS INTO THE 21ST CENTURY

In life it is inevitable to face new and ever growing challenges. To lead into the future there must be some guideposts, suggestions, for the days ahead. There are so many resources. It would be difficult to list everything, so I end the chapter by sharing the following few secrets or techniques that will help to keep a leader directed in these challenging times. [20]

1. ***Integrity*** must be placed first. Integrity will make or break you as a person; it will also make or break you as a leader, and it affects every area of life. It is not uncommon to read about gross accounting irregularities that produced astounding profits in major corporations. Somewhere, company leadership (or the individual involved) made a choice between the presence/absence of integrity. The person who is respected at the end of a career, no less a life, may not always be the most popular. Neither does integrity bring with it an easy path. But integrity brings a standard to the way life is lived and leadership is accomplished. Decisions made in integrity will not always be the most convenient, but they will be appropriate for the long term. Be consistent in your actions, whether it is with management, your team, or your family.

2. ***Decisiveness*** is necessary in leadership. Decisive people make the decision and take action. Decisive people are the opposite of those who never get quite enough information—those that analyze what information they do have and then move to take it to yet another committee. They wait for the 'perfect time' to make the decision only to find that the perfect timing never comes. Among the worst qualities to show a team is that of

indecision. The ability to be decisive will be critical in any situation calling for leadership, to make the decision and go for it. Leaders make decisions based on past experience and ready information, and put that decision into action. Their ability to do so encourages those around them to grow, adapt, and develop.

3. **Visionary** leaders have the ability not only to see what is in the present - anyone can do that – but also the ability to glimpse the future. Outstanding leaders in every arena not only see the team for what it can do now, but what it can become. Constantly assessing and coaching the team members toward the vision is inherently understood, almost second nature to the leader.

When a wise leader has a meeting, three things are generally on the agenda: team vision, mission, and goals. After the mission and goals are explained, the motivation portion of the meeting ties into the vision. When someone has a vision they understand that everything ties into it. And they know the value of taking time to develop the team members' personal visions and show them how to accomplish personal goals by tying into the overall vision. Consistently communicating vision provides the sense of moving with purpose. When people feel they are personally making a difference, it encourages and spurs them on to achieve goals sooner. Vision is critical for the future.

4. ***Knowledge*** is also critical as change happens faster and faster, moment by moment. But it is extremely important that it be the knowledge to master these changes, not just knowledge for the sake of knowledge. Having the right answer is not the whole of what will be needed; having the right answer faster than before is what we need today. Leadership requirements in the 21st century demand acquiring the skills to find the right answers, faster. With the Internet, classroom and online training, mentors, etc., knowledge is at our fingertips. The need for information, facts and comprehension will cause a leader to challenge team members and followers to use resources to acquire the knowledge necessary to master challenges. By acquiring appropriate knowledge, you will be able to navigate through the ocean and be at much greater advantage to achieve goals.

5. **Unselfishness** in words and actions will certainly be part of 21st century leader's portfolio. Stephen Covey, in his successful book *Seven Habits of Highly Effective People*, wrote that a true leader must be a servant to the ones he or she leads. The leader must be able to "give of oneself for the good of the team."

Being unselfish is definitely a choice. Certainly, it is not a character trait that is always easy to exhibit, but for excellence in the future it is not optional. How then? Be unselfish in praise of others, especially in

It is said that leaders lead by example and that actions speak louder than words. Do we have to look for the perfect leader? Is there a perfect leader after all?

public. Be unselfish with the time that it takes to be helpful; it may be costly, but it's absolutely necessary.

A recent survey said that the average management time invested doing "pure listening" with employees during the year is a mere two hours -- just two hours! 'Pure' listening time is that which is given with eye contact, acknowledgement and an absence of interruptions, including answering phone calls while listening, or speaking with another person, etc. You must be unselfish in your ability to help your team and followers, whether by the willingness to assist readily with a difficult phone call, jump in and remove road blocks for team members, or just 'be there' for a team member during challenging moments.

Reputable leadership training materials today emphasize that the way we treat people is enormously more important than what we pay them or how lavishly we furnish their offices.

Appreciation cannot be underrated!

VV, Paul Rom. Follow me as I follow Christ ...
unselfish Service.

1. How can we ~~want~~ destinguish between our desire, and God's vision for a specific task?

2. Being in ministry, effect our spiritual life ☺?

3. What can be done in order to ~~keep~~ on guard our relationship with the Lord?

4. Can our weaknesses herin our ~~leadership~~ work + reputation? (In my weakness you show yourself strong).

73

It's not fair to ask of others
what you are not willing to do
yourself
-Eleanor Roosevelt

We make a living by what we get.
We make a life by what we give.
-Winston Churchill

Ability is what you're capable of
doing. Motivation determines what
you do. Attitude determines how
well you do it.
- Lou Holtz

Chapter Five
Practicing Servant Leadership

I wonder about future leaders; how will they be identified, developed and prepared to face the multiple challenges that face them not only today, but tomorrow? Too many leaders are acting as managers (in a narrow sense) and merely coping. The potential exists for greatness, but it is often considered a nuisance to develop leadership character and skills.

Great leaders, and those teachable ones that will develop in leadership, that give to others of themselves in areas of influence, will in some way find themselves following a solitary path. These are the ones who will pursue a vision as a personal mission. They will tackle conflict and change. They will desire to finish the course, even if at times they walk alone.

Imagine how strong corporations, community service organizations, or families would be if competent leaders, those who are determined to develop and stay the course, were serving them all. This will only happen, yes, if leaders desire excellence and will work to shape and pursue a vision. But they must understand that creating the vision is only the beginning. The next challenge comes in identifying the strategy that should be applied to turn the vision into reality.

Leaders who want to be noted for excellence will discover their own vision and strengths. No one can be an excellent leader by trying to become, or impersonate, another. Nor is a leader with a vision necessarily someone with a brute force personality. Vision is not about personality, it is about being valuable to others. I want to prompt your thinking: how would you become an excellent leader?

There are many possible answers to this question, and there is not space to share them all. Ultimately, I believe when someone wants to be excellent in leadership, they will build first from their inner potential, then embrace a plan for success and pursue the competency required to lead.

LEADERSHIP TRUTH:
A leader has his own vision,
not a copy of someone else's.

LEADERS BUILD FROM INNER POTENTIAL

Leadership with excellence does not mean that the full impact of that leadership is felt immediately or even in the near future. To the contrary, that is not the goal. Rather each person, if they would live up to their potential, has the responsibility to find and complete their purpose in life and lead in whatever areas to which they are called. True leadership will have a lasting impact because of the vision of the leader. Ultimately, most excellent leaders have that reputation because someone identified their strengths and then encouraged and invested in them. It might be said that leaders who leave behind a legacy were enabled to do so by inter-action at some point in time with someone who modeled for them life skills and leadership patterns.

An excellent leader will build from their inner potential by first recognizing the value of others, particularly the value of those who have sacrificed time and energy to help them develop. Remember, there is a difference between a leader and a manager. A leader who will effect the days ahead for the positive will not operate from within a framework of methodology alone, but will also recognize the investment others have made in their life. In turn, these leaders will empower others.

LEADERS EMBRACE A PLAN FOR SUCCESS

Here is a hard truth: leadership does not mean there are always immediate followers. When a leader pursues excellence it may require that they stand alone in times of decision and crisis. But a plan for success will eventually bring others around to a helpful position, when it is offered. *Servant-leadership* skills will usher us into the competency to lead in the 21st century.

LEADERSHIP TRUTH:
The great leader is a servant first!

Think of the big picture for practicing excellent leadership and ask: how do I learn to lead for the benefit of whatever arena I am placed in? There is the need for a better approach to leadership, one that puts serving others including employees, customers, and community, as the number one priority. A helpful and holistic approach to work is *servant-leadership,* which emphasizes increased service to others, thus promoting a sense of community, and the sharing of power in decision making.

Generally, the corporate world has thought of the words *servant* and *leader* as being opposites. The definition of a paradox is when two opposites are brought together in a creative and meaningful way. So the words *servant* and *leader* have been brought together to create the paradoxical idea of servant-leadership.[21]

Obviously, a servant-leader is a servant first. Robert K. Greenleaf has written, "It begins with the natural feeling that one wants to serve, to serve first. Then conscious choice brings one to aspire to lead. The difference manifests itself in the care taken by the servant--first to make sure that other people's highest-priority needs are being served. The best test is this: Do those served grow as persons? Do they, while being served, become healthier, wiser, freer, more autonomous, more likely themselves to become servants?

Fundamentally, servant-leadership is a long-term, transformational approach to life and work. It is a way of being that has the potential for creating positive change throughout our society.

The concept of servant-leadership is having a growing impact on society. Many individuals and organizations have adopted servant-leadership as a guiding philosophy. As the premise that every individual has leadership abilities is accepted, this concept helps to enable personal growth; spiritually, professionally, emotionally, and intellectually. The ideas of M. Scott Peck, author of *The Road Less Traveled*, Parker Palmer, *The Active Life*, and others who have written on expanding human potential, add further support to this thought.

LEADERSHIP TRUTH:
Leadership seeks opportunities to both serve and lead.

The potential to raise the quality of life in society is a particular strength of servant-leadership as it encourages everyone to actively seek opportunities to both serve and lead others. Seeing the worth of this approach, an increasing number of companies have adopted servant-leadership as part of their corporate philosophy, or as a foundation for their mission statement. Among these are excellent examples of the Toro Company (Minneapolis, Minnesota), Synovus Financial Corporation (Columbus, Georgia), ServiceMaster Company (Downers Grove, Illinois), the Men's Wearhouse (Fremont,

California), Southwest Airlines (Dallas, Texas), and TDIndustries (Dallas, Texas).

Using the example of TDIndustries as an illustration, the belief that managers should serve their employees became an important value for the company. Servant-leadership is the company's guiding philosophy, and TDI began to include that concept in every facet of corporate life and training. Even today, any person within the company who supervises even one person is required to go through training in servant-leadership. Further, all new employees continue to receive a copy of "The Servant as Leader", and TDIndustries has developed elaborate training modules designed to encourage the under-standing and practice of servant-leadership."[22]

Servant-leadership materials are being used in corporate education and training programs as many management and leadership consultants utilize the concept as part of their ongoing work with corporations. Organizations are discovering that servant-leadership can truly improve how business is developed and conducted, while still successfully turning a profit.

Traditional theories of leadership are limited by a narrow focus on the relationship between managers and subordinates. The sharper distinction between the idea of a simple manager and a leader is clearly exhibited in servant-leadership. Because leadership is not to be understood as a particular type of person or position of authority, but rather the innate qualities that every individual possesses, the person exercising true leadership will illustrate the thought patterns and practices associated with leadership irrespective of position or placement in the structures of authority.

The leader has been perceived at times as the hero, or a visionary cheerleader. Of course everyone admires heroes, but it is easy to overlook the fact that some leaders are effective without being either obviously visionary or even particularly inspiring. There must be a place for leading by example and other forms of quiet leadership. Servant-leadership most aptly embodies this principle. Remember that we have established that the leadership spirit is part of the individual identity of every person. As the occasion arises, the individual chooses whether or not to lead. Within every person is something that is valuable to others. If allowed, it will influence, no matter the personality style.

We are now in a knowledge driven economy, a major change in the world in the last forty or more years, which is yielding a different understanding of leadership. First there were managers, supplemented at times by inspirational, visionary (heroic) leadership brought in to save the day. In this context, the *aim* of leadership was to produce organizational change, the *means* was to direct and motivate employees with an inspirational vision of a better future. The visionary was the point man; he or she stood alone. Today's leader, however, is servant visionary, possessing a vision for others.

LEADERS PURSUE COMPETENCY TO LEAD

We may recognize that potential for leadership is innate, and we may embrace servant-leadership as a plan for developing excellence; still it takes work to advance these ideas and move them into the realm of the practical. There is a pursuit to leadership, a competency that is required.

In today's increasingly knowledge-driven society, a different sort of leadership is required. Servant-leadership does embrace the concept that everyone has leadership potential in some area. This is not built on the force of per- sonality. The model of the hero striding onto the large stage gives a distorted view of what leadership really means; rather, consider the leadership concept of influencing others to accept a different idea or new way of looking at things. Whenever you are in a meeting with others, whether they report to you or not, and you convince them to adopt your idea of how to proceed on any topic, you are demonstrating thought-leadership. Such leadership is not a position; it shifts continuously around the table.

LEADERSHIP TRUTH:
Servant-leadership implies that every human has a seed of greatness needed by the world.

Leadership has always had something to do with providing direction. Therefore leaders, as we continue to push, must have a vision, a sense of direction. Sometimes they must stop and do the work to develop that vision and direction. Again, it is not about the force of personality. As a leader there will be something that others see as valuable. People will seek leadership that helps with direction. They will seek out the style of leadership that embraces the needs of followers, considers them and then encourages that they reach their full potential, thereby allowing them to perform at their best.

There are many who long to improve the human condition, and the servant-leader approach to leadership, structure, and decision making can provide a basis from which individuals can help to advance how others – those who do the work - are treated. Servant-leadership is more inclusive and truly offers hope and guidance for the days ahead in human development and for the creation of better, more caring institutions. Shifts in societal norms and expectations have mandated this; leaders cannot expect people to walk in one mindset for their own lives and embrace another paradigm at work!

So what is servant-leadership: a great idea or a contradiction in terms? The essential idea is that the leader serves the people he/she leads.

What do Servant-leaders do? [23]

- Devote their efforts to serving the needs of others through discovery of personal purpose, gifts and talents.
- Serve for the betterment of humanity.
- Focus on meeting the needs of those they lead.

- Develop others, encouraging them to bring out their best; the maximization of self.
- Facilitate personal growth which, in turn, is enacted in others.
- Listen to others and build a sense of community.

A leader is never truly a leader until they take the responsibility to go and do. Servant-leadership provides the opportunity to be an excellent leader if the challenge is taken. To lead for the benefit of others and do it is a service to all. Again, this philosophy expresses the idea that everyone was designed and born to serve with innate gifts and talents. There is a seed of greatness in everyone; it is his gift to the world.

But servant-leadership is not just about what is done, it is also about who the person is. A servant-leader, as an excellent leader:

- Seeks to discover one's own purpose, innate gifts and talents.
- Desires to use those gifts to serve mankind, while being prepared to serve at any and every opportunity.
- Is authentic, and displays authority.
- Is not competitive because of conviction.
- Pursues a deliberate vision in order to serve others.[24]

The 1990s witnessed lapses in ethics and the rise of arrogance among senior executives in many companies of disturbing magnitude; Enron and WorldCom were two notable examples, but not the whole story. Such events probably accelerated and deepened growing sentiment among many that interrelationships among leadership, character, and values ought to be made more significant. The integrity and character of leaders has been called into question. If the concepts of servant-leadership are followed there will be some natural results that will discourage such violation of leadership principles.

The servant-leader is not a copy of anyone else. When the principles of this philosophy are set in motion, an authenticity, authority and authorization to lead are released. The premise of conduct not betraying of oneself is manifested rather than the usual, insecure, power-hungry maneuvering.

A brief synopsis of the characteristics of the servant-leader and their development might be defined as follows. These, coupled with the list in chapter three of characteristics needed to lead into the 21st century, provide an excellent overview of a leader for the times.[25]

1. *Listening*. Leaders have always been valued for communication and decision making skills. While these are also important skills for the servant-leader, they need to be reinforced by a deep commitment to listening intently to others. He or she seeks to listen receptively to what is being said. Listening, coupled with regular periods of reflection, is essential to the growth of the servant-leader.

2. ***Empathy.*** The servant-leader strives to understand and empathize with others. People are seeking to be accepted and recognized for their special and unique spirits. It is a need. Therefore, good intentions of co-workers are assumed and they are not rejected, even if it is necessary to refuse to accept their behavior or performance.

3. ***Healing.*** So many today have broken spirits, emotional wounds and have suffered from a variety of other hurts. Blatantly, the difference between a traditional managerial role and a leader is displayed when the (servant) leader opens the way in doing his part to help heal. The search for wholeness is something servant-leadership seeks, not only to in order to help heal others, but also as a priority for the self to also be healed. Opportunities are sought to 'help make whole' those with whom the servant-leader comes in contact.

4. ***Awareness.*** Self-awareness strengthens the servant-leader. It is important to understand issues involving ethics and values. It lends itself to being able to view most situations from a more integrated, holistic position. Awareness causes the able leader to be disturbed by what is happening in the world around him.

5. ***Influence.*** Rather than relying on positional authority in making decisions, servant-

leaders have primary reliance on influence. Rather than coerce compliance, the servant-leader seeks to convince others. This particular element offers one of the clearest distinctions between the traditional, authoritarian model and that of servant-leadership. The servant-leader is effective at building consensus within groups.

6. *Conceptualization.* Servant-leaders seek to nurture the ability to "dream great dreams." To be able to look at any situation, problem, organization or team and perceive the possibilities requires being able to think beyond day-to-day realities. Servant-leaders seek discipline coupled with practice, to balance conceptual thinking and a day-to-day focused approach. Servant-leaders want to lead others to dream, and then believe sufficiently to experience the dream.

7. *Foresight.* To understand lessons from the past, realities of the present and possible consequence of a decision for the future: this is foresight. Until recently, here has not been much study on this topic; however, it would seem that having foresight is necessary to the intuitive leader.

8. *Stewardship.* Stewardship, as a key component of servant-leadership, assumes first and foremost a commitment to serving the needs of others, for the benefit of others. This spirit embedded in the pursuit of stewardship principles corresponds to the ability and

desire of an individual to always come through: the job *will* be well done. It will be thoroughly attended to because the character of the true steward mandates it to be so.

9. ***Commitment to the growth of people.*** Servant-leaders believe that people have value beyond tangible contributions. The responsibility is embraced to do everything possible to nurture their growth. Therefore, the servant-leader is deeply committed to the growth of each and every individual within the institution.

10. ***Building community.*** The servant-leader senses that much has been lost in recent human history as a result of the shift from local communities to large institutions as the primary shaper of human lives. This aware-ness causes the servant-leader to seek to identify some means for building community among those who work within a given institution. Servant-leadership suggests that true community can in fact be a reality, fighting the opinions of skeptics, believing it a possibility within every environment.

Robert K. Greenleaf, founder of Greenleaf Center for Servant-leadership said: "*All that is needed to rebuild community as a viable life form for large numbers of people is for enough servant-leaders to show the way, not by mass movements, but by each servant-leader demonstrating his own unlimited liability for a quite specific community-related group.*"

This is not a complete list of the characteristics of servant-leadership, but they help to identity the possibilities that this concept offers to those who are open to its invitation and challenge.

A final thought in the pursuit of this paradigm: the building of competency as a servant-leader is pertinent and vital. Ultimately, whatever style of leadership is adhered to, it must be grounded in the leader's moral character. Trustworthiness, reliability, respect of others, fairness, to name a few qualities, are all of increasing interest in the study of leadership. Though somewhat difficult to define, discovering quality values and choosing to act them out is most needed in the years ahead. A leader's concern for the greater good may represent the single most critical quality of leadership for the 21st century.

vv. Last Supper.

1. Are we concerned for God to approve our work or for others to like us? (75)

2. The perfect imitation of Christ would be the capable leader, or the servant leader. Can these two types of leader be separately? (83) Pg. 82

3. Being a visionary leader, does it mean to choose the Right followers? Is it a plan for success because of Godly example or for counting on particular people?

Reflection: Jesus was our perfect example of servant-leader. If He had come today, he would have done the same. Serving others like they were more imp. than himself was his goal. This should be our inspiration as well.

*Keep your dreams alive,
understand that to achieve anything
requires faith and belief in yourself,
vision, hardworking, determination
and dedication. Remember that all
things are possible for those who
believe.*
-Gail Devers

*Vision is the art of seeing
what is invisible to others.*
-Jonathan Swift

*Where there is no vision,
the people perish.*
-King Solomon

Chapter Six
Vision and Strategic Foresight

In a glimpse at economic, societal and environmental trends for the short and near-range future, the following might be forecast:

- The world's population will grow to 9.2 billion by 2050.
- The elderly population will grow dramatically throughout the world.
- The growth of information industries will create a knowledge dependant global society.
- Mass migration will redistribute the world's population.
- Militant Islam will spread and gain in power.
- Societal values will continue to change rapidly.
- Young people will place ever-increasing importance on economic success.
- Family structures will become even more diverse.
- The continuing urbanization will aggravate most environmental and social problems. [26]

According to Jay Gary in an article entitled, "Leading from the Future," he states that, on average, corporate management devotes 90% of their time on the "Inside and Now," leaving 10% of their energy to focus on the "Outside and Then."[27]

With the 'urgent' occupying so much con-
centration and energy, limited resources mean
that these percentages are probably even less in
the non-profit or small business sectors. It is
important to strengthen today's procedures but
it is no substitute for creating tomorrow's
programs. With this understanding comes a
pertinent question: How can we lead with our
eyes on the future, rather than the past?

Any organization that expects to move to the
next level, or expects to increase relevance and
productivity, must have what may be termed
"strategic foresight." Simply put, it is a
leadership quality that seeks to identify the
uncertainties and trends that affect future
actions. Planning for the future is thereby
effectively enabled.[28]

Australian educator Richard Slaughter defines
foresight as "the ability to create and maintain a
high-quality, coherent and functional forward
view, and to use the insights arising in
organizationally useful ways." The prevailing
pattern for leadership now, however, is based on
how the world is viewed at present. Performance
and evaluation are based upon that view as the
prevailing scale of measurement. Therefore, how
things have operated in the past will bring (or
not bring) future successes in similar measure
as the same pattern is maintained.[29]

With strategic foresight in mind, skillful
leadership will encourage the development of a
new set of suppositions based on current change

in the area of work or interest. This is not a traditional belief, rather an emerging view of how capabilities and the audience might change in ten years or so. While the goal is to preserve the benefit of the current, traditional model in use, the aim is to shift the organization to match future realities. Appreciate the past and the present, but look to the future.

When asked for the secret to his goal-scoring success, Canadian hockey player Wayne Gretsky expressed the essence of strategic foresight: "*I don't skate to where the puck is. I skate to where the puck is going to be.*"

VISION AND STRATEGIC FORESIGHT

Generally, when an event is reviewed through the lens of hindsight, almost always areas will be found where better decisions could have been made. Commonly the saying is heard, "If I knew then what I know now, I could have . . ." Of course, if an event that is in the past is evaluated, it is much easier to see where better decisions could have been made. There is no going back, though, and so strategic foresight is critical to help prepare for the future. To pre- pare for how that future might unfold.

One might ask if strategic foresight and vision are the same. In a more academic sense, strategic foresight might best be described as both a.) the formulation of emerging themes, issues, patterns and opportunities through the intuitive and creative exploration of external influences (e.g. environment, resources and competitive landscape) and b.) the formal composition of distinct steps, each delineated by checklists and supported by techniques for implementation through detailed attention to objectives, budgets, programs and operating plans.[30]

Strategic foresight concentrates on anticipating those forces that may come into play to assist and/or detract from a desired outcome. Slaughter, in his book *The Foresight Principle*, writes: "foresight is not the ability to predict the future. It is a human attribute that allows us to weigh up pros and cons, to evaluate different courses of action and to invest in possible futures." Slaughter suggests that the process of strategic foresight includes broadening our perceptions of what future possibilities may unfold and therefore, begin considering various situations beyond our normal line of sight.[31]

Vision, however, is less about this analysis and more about the intended result. Certainly, the two work together. No plausible vision can be formulated without a degree of foresight (or at least a concerted effort to possess it), and no vision can be achieved without the foresight to deal with the oncoming challenges and changes that stand between now and the fulfillment of vision. Strategic foresight, on the other hand, is just idle information if it has no vision directing it. The two possess a dynamic relationship.

There is scientific evidence that as humans, we are driven to want to know the future. Drs. Calvin and Ingvar, neurobiologists, have stated the human brain is hardwired in its drive to envision and plan for future events. The human brain is "capable of planning decades ahead, able to take account of extraordinary contingencies far more irregular than the seasons." But, strategic foresight, contrary to predicting the future, centers on the principle of evaluating the past and planning for an anticipated future, while still working in the present. It is not merely day dreaming, peering into the future, but intellectually reviewing and then carefully anticipating.

Do leaders need to be concerned with strategic foresight? Yes, because without foresight, we are apt to steer into the future blindly; unable to visualize the total picture and the possible consequences of our actions or inactions. Everyday unveils evidences of poor, strategic foresight. Year after year in the place that I live, I have watched as cars and motorcycles cruise past stop signs as though they do not exist. My constant observation has been, "If only they would enforce the laws about stop signs, certainly it would forestall a wreck." But nothing happens, and as traffic accidents inevitably begin to mount, the laws begin to be enforced.

If strategic foresight is considered a critical leadership quality then effort must be made to help a leader develop and refine this skill. Some suggested steps include:

- Understanding where you are today and assessing the implications of present actions and decisions.[32]
- Outlining possible future events which include both favorable, unfavorable and status-quo scenarios.[33]
- Establishing markers within your plans to help indicate which scenario might be unfolding.[34]

In further understanding the strategic foresight necessary for leadership, consider the following analogy. It required many more soldiers to take Normandy Beach in World War II than the number it took to accurately predict that Normandy was the best place to launch an invasion against German forces. Generally, it does take more people to conquer the hill than it takes to accurately predict which hill to conquer. There are more people good at producing results in the short term than there are visionary strategists. In other words, leaders must be developed that can think and function for the tomorrows that will come. Many leaders (and therefore their organizations) do quite well in the today, but what to do tomorrow?

Generally, leaders of today expend significant energy building strong and persuasive strategic visions to inspire and guide organizations into the future. Some leaders however, will be unprepared to cope with the future they have led into, or are so trying to lead, unless they prepare now and anticipate the ways in which that future might unfold. "If you don't know where you are going, you are bound to get there," someone has said. Vision is necessary. If you know where you are going, but you don't know what you will encounter there, you are equally challenged.

> **LEADERSHIP TRUTH:**
> **Strategic Vision plans for the future.**
> **Strategic Foresight anticipates and plans for the changes in that future.**

Vision will help a leader dream and plan for the future; strategic foresight will enable a leader to deal with the inevitable variations that will occur as that future unfolds. Therefore, while vision will always portray an image of the idealistic future, scenario planning will outline possible alternative results that the future may hold. It is the no-head-in-the-sand method of leadership. Understandably, innumerable possibilities for an alternate future exists, therefore leaders would do well to add strategic foresight to their vision framework.

The following thought is borrowed from the book, *Strategic foresight: The power of standing in the future.*[35]

> "When we truly 'stand in the future' we are able to create a view that is unrestricted by the present. We are free to create scenarios of possibility

and understanding. We are free to realize that the future is not pre-determined, something that we have to react to and cope with - but rather that it offers a range of possibilities, depending on our responses now to those possibilities."

> ***LEADERSHIP TRUTH:***
> ***Leaders are meant to be out front.***
> ***They are indeed people of vision.***

Definitely then, strategic foresight and vision are distinct and complementary components of a leader's repertoire for the 21st century and beyond. But to conclude this chapter, I want to address vision as a single, foundational thought in which these two components converge. We can call it *strategic vision.*

STRATEGIC VISION

Leaders are meant to be out front. They take followers to places they would not otherwise tend to go on their own. And the only way they do this is to see farther and a little bit sooner down the road than others generally do. A great example of this was Martin Luther King, Jr. His life inspired a generation of African Americans, and others who were keen to hear his message of hope. His vision was of a land where freedom would ring true for every person that made that land his home. His words of challenge are legendary:

"I have a dream that one day this nation will rise up and live out the true meaning of this creed: We hold these truths to be self –evident: that all men are created equal ...that day when all of God's children, black men and white men, Jews and Gentiles ...will be able to join hands and sing in the words of the old Negro spiritual, 'Free at last! Free at last! Thank God almighty, we are free at last ...'"[36]

Though his vision of a better world is not yet fully realized and it cost him his life, it did bring freedom to another level and changed the fabric of America. He was a man with a vision, a powerful vision, a contagious vision. His partners in the civil rights movement, having been inspired by this powerful ideal, had much work to do. The ebb and flow of America's equality movement have been many and at times severe. The vision showed the way. The strategy lived and continues to live out his vision.

LEADERSHIP TRUTH:
Vision is having a clear picture of the future and the belief that it can be realized.

Visionaries must be able to get ordinary people to do the extraordinary. But, as with any leadership quality, you cannot be so far separated from the followers that you lose impact. This is because vision *does* have the ability to inspire followers.

A leader may need to understand accounting procedures, he may need to have a good handle on administrative skills, and a plethora of other qualities, but it will be the communication of vision that attracts others. People ultimately care more about leadership than management.

The word "vision" has been overused in recent time, in my opinion, and has brought a sense that someone cannot be a leader if he is not visionary by nature. The plethora of writing in the subject during the 90's did much to aid this. But this is not true. Remem-ber, everyone has the potential for leadership. In the book *Built to Last,* the myth of the visionary is dispelled as the authors relate their study of eighteen companies that were effective for more than fifty years. None of the companies were led by entrepreneurial visionaries but rather by leaders who were committed to building a visionary company.[37] It could be accomplished through leadership that allowed the vision to take place. The importance of vision lies in the team as a whole, not necessarily just in the leader. The primary leader may not be the originator of all vision, but he will be personally and thoroughly tied to the vision.

LEADERSHIP TRUTH:
In the journey toward fulfilling a vision, there will be those who hope you fail.

Vision can lift us up in courage to accomplish the impossible. The loss of heart happens when there is no leadership to prop up the process. A leader with vision can incur defeats and set backs but still maintain a sense of faith that, in spite of opposition, success will come.

When vision is embraced, a dedication to the *fulfillment* of the vision is birthed. At that point, it will have effect on followers. Men and women of leadership ability can help lift up people to great heights, heights they would not normally obtain by themselves.

Again, this is because a leader tends to see farther than others do, and before others do. I have an acquaintance that has a severe physical condition that can be improved through regular physical exercise. However, due to a weight condition and a mind-set that she couldn't exercise, she refused to even try. Her boss was an exercise advocate who had overcome extreme physical difficulties. Because my friend was inspired by the life of her boss, she wanted to be like him; she started regular walking and strength training. Her leadership pushed her harder than she would have pushed herself. The result was better personal conditioning than she had experienced in a lifetime!

Vision makes the impossible seem possible.

Vision has a lot to do with this process of convincing people to do what they previously thought impossible. A visionary leader may not have all the conventional training that seems appropriate, but again, with an abundant dose of vision, followers are still inspired. The Russian poet Boris Pasternak said, "It is not revolutions and upheavals that clear the road to new and better days, but someone's soul inspired and ablaze."

How do leaders go about making vision known? How can they get the vision from the realm of ideas and into the realm of activity? The following three headings are worth heeding as steps to lead your team into the future.

- Uncover the vision.
- Unveil the vision.
- Unleash the vision.

Uncovering the Vision

Any seasoned hunter would tell you that, when the hunt is on, the aim is to get your prey! You search for it based on historical patterns. Experience tells you where the catch usually is found. But once found, the past and immediate position of your prey is no longer the issue. When it is time to shoot, you do not aim for where the animal has been or is now, but for where it will be at the point of impact. Strategic thinking about vision suggests we must act in advance of the critical changes taking place in our environment.

A leader's vision is not only about the work that is to be done. It will include his personal vision, based on his personality, gifts, experiences and passion: the place that he purposes to reach as a person. The second part is organizational vision, that of the group with which he works. Public vision is not to be found where no personal vision exists. Can you articulate your vision? If so, good for you. If not, think.

Decide first where you want to go; put it down on paper clearly. This is your vision statement. Do you know, have you questioned yourself for your leadership values? Discovering the vision is a process. It will not come as handwriting on the wall. Commit yourself to thoughts of where you and your organization should be in fifteen years. This must be more than a dream; it's a commitment to put all necessary effort into seeing its realization.

Next, when it comes to corporate vision, don't be sidelined by errors in thinking. Leaders sometimes believe that vision must come from them and them alone. The best vision casting for a corporate unit is done by the corporate group. This is the reason we have used the title, "uncovering the vision," as opposed to "creating the vision." Why? Genuine vision is most often revealed through teamwork, the synergy of a group inspired by their leader. Remember no one person has the corner on truth, experience, wisdom or insight.

Effective leaders today share ownership—share creation—of the vision with his or her team. The team has ideas that develop the dream. And the

103

team must be enlisted to do the work of realizing the dream.

LEADERSHIP TRUTH:
Broad goal ownership equals support
for the leader.

Do not be fooled, though. There is no free ride, no relinquishing of responsibility that comes with team-building vision. The defining of mission is determined together by the organizational team in this scenario, but the leader must ultimately guide the group into fulfilling the mission. Collaborative development must still be guided by purposeful government.

Every organization, whether for-profit or not-for-profit, has a group of people with vested interest in it. They have tremendous emotional stakes in the success of that group, a deep sense of ownership. Therefore, the leader must respect the views of the other major leaders in the process of developing vision for the group. No, this is not chaos. Rather it is order, where key players have input and are listened to throughout the process of developing vision.

A servant-leader, as we have seen, values the team. Vision must be determined by the group, which provides safety from stagnation and failure. The group will monitor itself and give thought to the ongoing validity of the vision, and through strategic foresight measure the needs for its activation, making adjustments when and if necessary. Because it is not about an individual, the process remains fluid, dynamic and purposeful.

Unveiling the Vision

After the leadership team has decided the vision, that vision must be shouted from the house-tops... again, and again and again.

Unveiling the vision means getting it out of the stale pages of some core document and into the functional life of the organization. It means making it available—no, unavoidable—to the entire team. The challenge is given to everyone to memorize the vision statement. It is printed on brochures and coffee mugs, recited it at team meetings, etc.

These internal processes are so fundamental and vital to the quest for visionary success. The direction of the group as a whole must be communicated to every part.

To assume that your group knows where you are headed with them as a leader is a grave error; to assume that they innately understand the direction of the organization is naïve, at best. Everyone needs to be informed constantly of the big picture and helped to see where they fit individually. When they sense they belong, they will work to see the vision fulfilled.

In today's world, people respect individuals and groups that know where they are going and can show it. Skepticism and pessimism are the rules of the day. The public demands to know why you exist and what you hope to accomplish, no less the team. Give them the vision.

Unleashing the Vision

In one of the classic "Peanuts" cartoons, Lucy asks Schroeder, who is playing the piano, if he knows what love is. Schroeder stands at attention and begins to recite, "Love: a noun, referring to a deep, intense, ineffable feeling toward another person or persons." Then he sits down at his piano. The final frame shows Lucy saying with great disappointment, "On paper, he's great." Most vision and mission statement have the same problem: On paper they look great.

LEADERSHIP TRUTH:
A leader makes the vision happen in real life. It must be unleashed beyond the paper.

A basic fact of vision is that is must be achievable. Not in the present, but there must be the hope that it will come to pass. Leadership must devote itself to the issues of goals and strategies, continually asking, "Where do we go next and, realistically, how do we get there?"

It cannot be reiterated enough that everything in the group or organization should be evaluated in context of the vision. There may be programs that must be relinquished in order to achieve the vision because they keep us preoccupied with minute, meaningless tasks. They divert us from the goal.

Always the goal is to keep on track, focused on the purpose. Yes, re-evaluation is sometimes necessary, but ultimately, fulfilling the vision is the goal. If maintenance of the status quo detours the journey, then remove those things that hinder. A group or company can become so busy with the present that they have no drive or ability to begin new initiatives toward fulfilling the vision. The leader must provide insurance against such negative momentum.

It is imperative to beware of the enemies of vision. They are always to be found, and they will work their way into your processes at some point. Again, it is left to the leader, possessing of vision and strategic foresight, to be a shepherd against them. Some that you will often hear noted include:

- **Tradition**: The way that we have always done it is the way to always stay the same. "Doing things the same way and expecting different results is the definition of insanity," someone has said. Pay heed.

- **Systems and programs**: The bureaucracy that exists in many organizations, not to mention stays ingrained in the minds of many leaders, is often nothing more than a dam set up to stop the flow of progress. Systems and programs must serve the vision; the vision must not be slave to the systems.

- **Lethargy**: It is often much easier to just stay the course than it is to make the necessary adjustments for dynamic movement. Vision is an "ends" statement. It has a destination in mind. But the paths to get there may have to be changed from time to time.

- **Prudence**: Not simply the same as caution, prudence is caution enshrined. Caution can be positive; no one wants to be reckless. But prudence, in this regard, relates more to that saying, "You old prude." It conveys the image of the one who will not be moved simply for the sake of not being moved, or simply because change is an evil to be resisted at all costs. Every organization has its prudes.

- **Immediacy**: Vision is a long term enterprise. It is very difficult to get to the end results if the affairs of the everyday and of the mundane are always getting in the way. Often, the important matters are offset by the urgent matters—even if the so-called urgent are less than important.

- **Tunnel vision**: Work is not only about work. Sounds odd, right? But still, it is true. The balanced life, not the one infected by an inability to escape work, is the one more likely to produce for the vision.

As a leader, one of your number one jobs is this thing of vision: to discover, craft and preach it, both within and without the organization. It is also then to lead the team into its discovery of that vision, and into the implementation of it through strategic thought and effectual conduct. Such use of vision will also attract quality people, and can be used like a yardstick to measure a group's progress. Finally, it is like a laser point-ing you to your destination. You know where you are going.

In pursuing the vision, you can keep the main things as the main things. And, you can look to the future.

LEADERSHIP TRUTH:
Vision is like glue. It holds the
group together.

VV. Flowers + God's will.

1. Looking to the future and planning for it, does it go against faith? No.

2. How much space should we allow for God in our future planning?

3 - Can following the vision pull us away from God + his vision?

Reflections: Strategic foresight + vision are necessary to effectively plan for the future. Even though vision is necessary, it has to be God's vision we pursue. When our vision is God's vision, then we plan for success.

"It takes 20 years to build a reputation and five minutes to ruin it."
– Warren Buffet.

You need to claim the events in your life to make yourself yours. When you truly possess all you have been and done, which may take some time, you are fierce with reality.
- Florida Scott-Maxwell

Sunlight is the best disinfectant.
- Jozef Imrich

There is no persuasiveness more effectual than the transparency of a single heart, of a sincere life.
- Joseph B. Lightfoot

Chapter Seven
Authenticity, Transparency and Character

" Let your yes, be yes and your no be no"
"The character of Christ, to be built in you".
" We are fearfully + wonderfully made".

Nothing is more important in the discussion of true leadership than that of character. Nothing is more important to, or reflective of, quality character than this aspect of transparency. "I am what I say I am." So, let's take a few moments to absorb these concepts into our pursuit of excellent leadership for the 21st century.

LEADERSHIP IS BIRTHED IN AUTHENTICITY

Authenticity is a key word for leadership. It is defined as, "coherence in performing a role and communication that has an underlying consistency, a thread of thought tying all things together".[38] More simply, it is consistency between words and deeds. It also includes, in my opinion, comfort with self.

Does this authenticity really have anything to do with leadership? Obviously, yes, because effective leaders are defined, and will be even more so as this century advances, not so much by individual, personal characteristic traits as by their ability to combine their strengths with a sense of what works naturally for them in their

111

dealings with others. They will be who they are, not a shadow of an ideal. The process will not be contrived.

LEADERSHIP TRUTH:
There can be no authenticity in leadership without a transparent leader

---

In order for leadership to rise to a place of impact, leaders must know how to engage with organizational life in a way that creates the legitimate possibility for healthy change. Such engagement presses an uncomfortable point: that of being a *transparent* leader. It seems only correct to me to assume that there can be no authenticity in the process of leading without transparency. It begs to be said that this is difficult in this day and age. In a time when there no longer seems to be a firm consensus on what constitutes right and wrong, it becomes easy to allow compromise and leniency in so many areas. Let us address this concern.

AUTHENTICITY ALLOWS TRANSPARENCY

A transparent leader must have the goal and vision to lead a transparent organization. Such a group would be rooted in an understanding of core value, based on the "greatest good for the greatest number of people". With a leader who believes in doing the right thing at all times, no matter what the consequences, it would seem inevitable to have accountability, openness and through them a great company.[39]

112

Arrogance in leadership has been all too ˌapparent lately. Many have attempted to lead with a maverick attitude of being the "answer man". "Just move over and watch me work!" But leadership is not a license to stride in and tell people what to do, with no willingness to have actions checked and challenged.

LEADERSHIP TRUTH:
Transparency in leadership builds trust; trust breeds confidence that results in productivity.

Leadership strengths and gifting will be born out through the seasoning that takes place over time. Character, however, is another story. One does not wait till the "one day" for it to appear. It is rather about the 'doing' of leadership day in and day out, refining oneself along the way.

Too many would-be leaders have copied stand-ards and practices that are not appropriate, standards and practices that almost guarantee non-performance. If leaders would measure their decisions, perhaps even their personalities, they would avoid much poor performance and conflict. Great teams, organizations, or groups cannot be built for the long term on force of personality; rather they must be built on trust. This does not mean that people will necessarily like one another all the time; but good leadership demands trust, and where trust exists there will be understanding.

Whatever their role in leadership, CEOs, principals, priests, and leaders of any type must develop a conscious sense of accountability, collaboration and inspiration that gives the people around them the ability to withstand difficult circumstances and setbacks. This openness shows personal confidence and yields equal confidence in followers that serves to bridge expectations and results. The performance of the followers is motivated and enabled. Such personal confidence will also serve as the balance between arrogance and despair during the course of interaction between the organization and its participants.[40]

Undoubtedly, a leader's personal self-confidence will build confidence in others through supportive behavior. The organization then, in turn, exercises confidence in itself, and this reinforces its accountability and innovation. Finally, people outside the organization or group will get on board because people naturally gravitate toward confidence. Authenticity and the transparency that it allows are the building blocks for this confidence.

CONFIDENCE BASED ON AUTHENTICITY IS THE ROAD TO EXCELLENCE

Good leadership will inherently strive against mediocrity. But when existing leadership is not challenged to authenticity and its resulting excellence, those being led will surrender to mediocrity. This is a trap leading to poor attitudes, responses, and generally a sense of doom that causes problems to actually be intensified.

For the sake of awareness, please note the following characteristics of a losing leader or organization.[41] Use them to evaluate your own position at the moment.

- Decreased communication
- Rampant criticism and blame
- Eroded respect
- Common occurrences of increasing isolation
- An inward-turning focus
- The development of small cliques and turf-guarding
- Paralyzed initiative
- Dying aspirations
- Contagious negativity

Constant failure tends to erode confidence and will naturally produce additional failure or loss. Confidence is not a secret formula to effective leadership, but it is a powerful key. Confidence is not arrogance, for the arrogant leader does not consider that he is accountable. Generally, such a leader does not work well with a team; rather, he demands to be served. An authentic, confident leader will try to support others throughout the organization and share inform-ation and authority. The goal is to move from strength to strength (adding the strength of each participant), thereby disabling failure through authentic, trustful team building.

Disciplines which are holistic in nature are required if leadership is to take a group or organization to victory rather than loss. Authentic character demands that there is no choice between reason and intuition, head and heart; they work together. No one chooses to walk on one leg alone, if the opportunity to walk on both legs is an option, it is said.

Effort, then, must be made to seize every opportunity to make determinations and decisions from a point of strength. And strength is birthed really only in this kind of integrity. To achieve a high performance level and satisfactory organizational culture, the road must *start* with leadership that is confident and transparent. Confident enough to be in public who they are in private, and transparent enough to let their works be seen by those who need to be led, so that they too may be encouraged to be authentic.

LEADERSHIP TRUTH:
Failure can only be turned to success when it is molded into useful lessons.

This kind of confidence also makes possible the common adage, *"failure breeds success."* The statement becomes a truism when we learn from failure. Authentic confidence allows the leader to take mistakes and mold them into useful lessons.

Stephen R. Covey in his *The 8th Habit: from Effectiveness to Greatness* aims to specifically spotlight the gap between effectiveness and greatness. In brief, he has suggested that when leaders find their voice and that of the organization, they must then help others discover their voice. Ultimately, it is a statement for building trust. Confidence cannot be built without trust.

AUTHENTICITY IS A WORK IN PROGRESS

All of this leads back to the beginning: authenticity, transparency and excellence must be working components for personal leadership to be functioning at its best. Personal leadership, or leadership of self, is not optional; the leader must first lead himself if he is to function in excellence. None of the characteristics that are necessary to leadership are built overnight. As the true self comes into being, everyone will reap the benefits.

LEADERSHIP TRUTH:
The person who cannot lead himself
cannot in turn lead others.

Why should there be personal leadership- that is, leadership of self? What are the benefits? I believe the following checklist—cherry-picked from a variety of sources—will be made evident in the person who is striving to lead in his personal life. It is not all-inclusive, but provides food for thought. Out of this anchoring of self, the strength to be an authentic leader of influence will be enhanced.

1. Since personal leadership makes things happen, it must be rooted in character. Character stands out.

2. As you strive to be the best you can be, the desire to enable others to be their best will emerge.

3. An attitude of service is your personal and organizational focal point.

4. There is confidence to act on what you know and believe to be true.

5. You know what you are talking about, but at the same time you approach others with an ear to learn from their life and experiences. You understand that learning is an ongoing process.

6. You approach every event and endeavor with passion / commitment.

7. It is a central motivation to help others grow and promote their success. You will not be myopic.

8. Simply – you approach all you do with the intention to do your best. You strive to keep improving, preparing for the next job.

9. You will keep learning; it is a fatal error to stagnate.

10. The mind, heart and spirit are regenerated, becoming receptive to new ideas, through vacation; you take vacations.

11. You benefit from being with people who are different from you, listening, evaluating, learning, open to critical thinking and others who can help you in this direction.

12. Family is central and should always be held in priority.

13. You believe and trust in people, setting the example for others to believe and trust in you.

It has been the common thought that the leader must attend the next 'cutting edge' conference to keep abreast of trends and ideas in personal development. But what then do you do when training and travel budgets are slashed, or there is no time for the next, new intensive leadership program? Is it always the next guru that must provide useful revelation (as useful as they may be)? We have said before that one of the greatest teachers is daily life, with its challenges, frustrations and opportunities. It can be used to evaluate and to learn. To do so, however, leaders must take a careful, honest look inward.

Frances Hasselbein, Leader of the Girl Scouts of America, has provided the following, simple advice for reshaping your own thought processes (personal development), and thereby inspire others to respond positively (leadership development). Remember these items:

- It is not about "I" – it's about "We".
- You don't lead from your desk.
- Throw out the hierarchical, demeaning language. For example, who aspires to be a "subordinate" or "at the bottom" of an organization?
- Leaders lead by inspiring and mobilizing people against a powerful mission/vision and

a couple of goals. You don't lead by giving orders.

- Personal discipline is having a "Not to Do List" and learning how to gracefully say "No".
- Leadership is a very personal thing; it is a definition of "how I want to be" versus "how I must do". It is character that really defines a leader.

Yes, you need to lead yourself before you can lead others. It is an essential part of your development. How can others be effectively led if personal confidence is waning, if there is no attitude of strength?

Dee Hock, an acclaimed leadership expert wrote, "It is management of self that should occupy 50 percent of our time and the best of our ability. And when we do that the ethical, moral, and spiritual elements of management are inescapable."[42]   Coupled with this is the idea purported in the book *Emotional Intelligence* by Daniel Goleman.[43]   Mr. Goleman has studied why some leaders develop to their fullest potential while others never quite develop at all.   He concluded that the difference is self-leadership. The terminology he uses is "emotional self-control." This form of self-control according to Goleman is exhibited when a leader perseveres despite opposition or discouragement; they stay focused and refuse to give up.

Mr. Goleman observed that exceptional leaders distinguish themselves because they "know their strengths, their limits, and their weaknesses."[44] No one can do the work of self leadership for you. It is accomplished alone and it is certainly not easy. Truthfully, it is easier to try to tell *others* how to do the work than it is to do the work of self development.

A *CEO Magazine* article observed that "the age of the imperial CEO (chief executive officer) is waning. In its place, a crop of new CEOs – humble, team building, highly communicative – are rising".[45] Similarly, one of the unexpected findings in the book *Good to Great* was of the universally modest and unassuming nature of CEOs in the good-to-great companies. This contrasts considerably with the self-promoting style of many popular business leaders in recent years. Despite celebrity status, many of these leaders typically did not have an enduring positive impact on their companies.

Bass and Steidlmeier, noted authors in the realm of ethical leadership, contend that transformational leadership is only authentic when it is grounded on the leader's moral character, concern for others, and consistency of ethical values with action. A leader's credibility and trustworthiness are critical, and increasing numbers make the case that character—as defined by qualities like one's striving for fairness, respecting others, humility, and concern for the greater good—represents the most critical quality of leadership. Much work is needed in the years ahead to assure greater clarity of concept of character. It must play a prominent role in leadership development practices in organizations.[46]

> ### LEADERSHIP TRUTH:
> ### The effective leader will be anchored by a healthy self-knowledge, birthed out of healthy self-examination.

If a leader is to actually lead the way, if he is to help people work in their strengths, if he is to influence organizations and their programs the leader must understand his or her own behaviors and emotions. He must work to develop them into patterns of authenticity and transparency that will allow him to have confidence in himself, to be open with his actions, and to influence others to do the same. This is a hefty step toward personal development.

Leadership author, Jo Ball, describes strong leadership as being about developing purpose and responsibility – purpose being meaning and direction, responsibility being 'ownership' and taking charge. And while good leaders will be in charge of their specialist area – the classroom, the office or the home – outstanding leaders will have defined their purpose in every area of their life, through home and career, right out into the community.[47] They will be developing in each of these areas, and using their experiences from each of them to learn.

- A leader needs to be beyond reproach. W.
Reflection: The Bible tells us that there remains nthg. hidden under the sun. No matter what we do it has consequences or it will reward us. In our work as leaders ours our reward comes from God and nthg. can be hidden from Him.

122

Can a healthy self-knowledge be birthed from knowing Biblical humility? Explain Biblical humility 2 parts (Yes.)

Should a healthy self-knowledge be confused with pride? No.

> *"If you would create something*
> *you must be something."*
> - Johann Wolfgang von Goethe

> *It is amazing how much you can*
> *accomplish when it doesn't matter*
> *who gets the credit.*
> - Anonymous

> *None of us is as smart as all of us.*
> - Ken Blanchard

1. In order for a team to successfully function, there needs to be trust. Keeping things hidden while leading a team, will it take that team on the extra level? No. What biblical example of transparency can we mention here? Jesus explaining the parables to his disciples.

How can "failure breed success" in our spiritual life with God? Repentance - definition- When you repent you have 'learned' your lesson + learned not to repeat it. (hopefully).

vv. Appointing deacon in early church.
vv. The salt of the earth.

Ret

We need to understand that in God we are different from the world and keep our diversity when mingleing with the world, when doing God's work we have to work tog, as one Body.

1. Could Christ have done a better job himself and not trusted his disciples and us with the Great Commission?
   Prob. Yes. But the example of the Unity wouldn't be clear in us.

2. Do we see the example of team work in the trinity?   Yes.

3. How did God create us for Community and not for lonelymess?
   Adam + Eve. The appointing of deacons

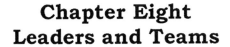

Chapter Eight
Leaders and Teams

Antoine de Saint Exupery has been quoted as saying that "If you want to build a ship, don't drum up the men to gather the wood, divide the work, and give orders. Instead, teach them to yearn for the vast and endless sea".[48]

In the past few decades a shift has occurred away from structures wherein managers tended to view people as tools, and organizations considered workers as cogs in a machine. Moving into the 21st century, organizations are moving from what could be called traditional, oppresssive, and hierarchical modes of leadership to leadership based on teamwork and community. This model seeks to involve others in decision making, and is strongly based in ethical and caring behavior, while also attempting to enhance the personal growth of people. The thought is that this approach will work to help improve the quality of organizations, institutions, and people, and the thought is probably correct.

Reviewing many of the writings being contributed on leadership at present (ex. Blanchard, Covey, Senge, Greenleaf, and others), reveals a shift in the understanding of leadership. It is no longer viewed from the traditional management angle, but rather to that

125

of service and personal growth. These views are having an increasingly profound effect on many who seek to lead others in excellence.

Leadership competency will always matter, but as the competitive environment changes, most organizations will not need the 'Lone Ranger' type of leader as much as a leader who can motivate and coordinate a team-based approach. In the future there will be greater uncertainty and many, if not all, aspects of leadership will require a more shared approach to leadership. The model of effective leadership in the future will be one of encouraging environments that unlock the entire organization's human asset potential.

LEADERSHIP TRUTH:
Leading into the future includes sharing the power.

In the world of instant access and immediate everything, leadership described as being from the top down is behind the times. Powerful leadership is no longer just about the boss; it is about the team, wherever that team is found, in the office, the classroom or at home. Living with the present tempo of life and moving ahead requires leaders to be people who also understand that every one of the team will be involved in some form of leadership. The leader that understands this becomes a powerful influencer, a leader that other leaders will strive to imitate.

People do not want to be driven. Powerful leaders are flexible, understanding that it's not about titles and position, but it is about knowledge and the best way to utilize that knowledge. Take for example, a jazz band moving into improvisation; at the moment of inspiration through a singular instrument a new theme or new song emerges. That instrument for that period of time is the conductor of the band, so to speak. The band leader allows the freedom, follows it, and directs it back into the whole. Influential leaders know that supporting the thoughts and feelings of staff encourages them to want to accomplish tasks. The freedom and inspiration of the moment drives them, as opposed to making them feel 'driven'.

GENUINE LEADERSHIP INCLUDES ENCOURAGING EVERYONE TO LEAD.

Leadership that is skillful flows within the group, bottom to top, top to bottom and side to side. At times those at the bottom will inspire as much as those at the top. A leader should strive to influence the group's vision so that each member will view themselves as part of the organizational whole.

LEADERSHIP TRUTH:
Any leader's first task is to build the leadership team.

To expect greatness of others requires a move beyond the fear of not knowing what to expect or how it will be accomplished, and toward an attitude of release. As greatness is expected, encouraged and allowed, everyone will desire to contribute their very best. In the future, a great leader may not have the most charisma in the bunch, nor may he be the best listener within the group, and he may not have a list of famous achievements; the great leader will be skilled at unleashing the talent of others.

A Scout leader was trying to lift a fallen tree from the path. His pack gathered around to watch him struggle. "Are you using all your strength?" one of the scouts asked. "Yes!" was the exhausted and exasperated response. "No, you're not using all your strength," the Scout replied. "You haven't asked us to help you."

Everyone on the team must be committed to the goals and objectives if success is desired, for sure. But they must also be *allowed* to be so committed.

A basic truth is that the effectiveness of a leader is largely dependent on those that he has gathered around him. This is the essence of mentoring a leadership team: one person empowers others by sharing through relationship and drawing out the resources of each team member.

Interaction with others on the team is a necessity; saying that everyone's ideas are welcome, but choosing not to hear those ideas, becomes destructive to the organization. Lip service destroys; genuine involvement adds life and vibrancy. Again, the key is to know that everyone on the team is essential.

If leadership is not just the responsibility of one individual, then it must be about constantly learning from and engaging others on the team; that means helping everyone understand their leadership role within the group.

THE DEVELOPMENT OF LEADERSHIP TEAMS

It is a fallacy to believe that leaders must know everything. They do not, nor should they be expected to, know everything. More importantly, they need to be resourceful. Leaders should know where and how to find the answers to issues that are pressing. They must share the vision, generate ideas and resolve problems through people. *"Leaders do not have to be great men or women by being intellectual geniuses or omniscient prophets to succeed, but they do need to have the "right stuff."*[49]

Finding the right participants to leadership can be one of our greatest challenges. A word of caution seems pertinent here: whenever possible, promote from within your group or organization. When people are passed over, the message that "you are not valued" is broadcast loud and clear. It may appear that present employees or group members are not as qualified as those on the outside. Any gains, however, will be strictly short term if it means that loyalty from your insiders is diminished or negated.

It is true that you get what you expect; leaders understand this. It's been said that people rise to the challenge when it is *their* challenge. The power of people to call on the gifts within and accomplish amazing things must not be under-estimated. As others are enabled to not only challenge processes, but to contribute ideas of their own, they are encouraged to be all they can be. It is not just about communicating the vision one possesses; it is about involving others in the formulation and ownership of the vision.

Team members will then recognize that it is safe to think creatively and to share those thoughts. An environment of encouragement is estab-lished, even allowing for mistakes. The team is genuinely built and encouraged to be one as each individual is viewed, legitimately, to have leadership potential. The demand for excellence from individuals is then realistic, because everyone is seen as able to make contributions to the organization. They sense it, and know it, and will be challenged to live up to it.

Leaders don't just empower, they breed a culture that grows the seeds of empowerment so that every employee or individual feels safe in making contributions to the organization, thereby em-powering themselves. A noted leadership coach says, "*You cannot be a great leader unless your confidence in others is as strong as your confidence is yourself.*"[50] Building relationships is vital to becoming a team. Leadership without a team is no longer leadership. Experts repeatedly state that we are moving into a time when group leadership is replacing individual leadership.

Warren Bennis, distinguished professor of business administration of the University of Southern California, has written that great groups make strong leadership teams. "Great groups make strong leaders. On the one hand, they're all non-hierarchical, open, and very egalitarian. Yet they all have strong leaders. That's the paradox of group leadership. You cannot have a great leader without a great group and vice versa. Great groups are the product of meticulous recruiting. Cherry-picking the right talent for a group means knowing what you need and being able to spot it in others. It also means understanding the chemistry of a group."[51]

> ## LEADERSHIP TRUTH:
> ### A leadership team is a partnership in success!

Teams are about relationship, and leaders work on building relationships. Enthusiasm for the vision or goal is useless unless excitement and enthusiasm is built around that vision. In short, leaders influence others to get needs met in support of the common goal. A quote from the Los Angeles Times Business Journal sums it up nicely, "To become a successful leader, you must be able to effectively self evaluate, to be able to step out of yourself on occasion and view your own behavior with objectivity. This enables you to make powerful and personal choices about how you relate to the people to whom you provide leadership."[52]

In developing the team, leadership development implies:

- The team must know where they are going. Leaders will learn how to define and cast a **vision** to give direction.

- As people follow the leader and pursue the vision, leaders must learn how to define and clarify **values**.

- Trust is essential for the team to be dynamic. Therefore, leaders must sustain the integrity of the **mission** of the organization.

- Any member of a team wants to know, "**How can I make a difference?**" Leaders must clearly communicate how individuals can be involved to answer this very important question.

- Leadership will understand how and when to **release the group for service**.

Teams are the vehicle of choice in today's organizations. Much research has demonstrated the superiority of group decision-making over that of even the most able individual in the group. Some mistakenly interpret "team based" organization to mean "work by committee."

However, the place of a leader and leadership duties is non-negotiable. The ground rules for team operation are established by the leader.

There are at least six leadership and team styles that have been used for years. We need to take a quick look at them: visionary, coaching, affiliative, democratic, pacesetting, and commanding. The following descriptions provide data adapted from the Hay Group, a global management consultancy, giving a brief review of each style and how each style works in a team setting.

Visionary style

A visionary leader communicates vision and gives clear direction. This helps people move toward a shared hope or dream. This is the classic model of leadership. The impact on the team is very positive. Clearly the team will know where they are going, but they will not know how they will get there. People are released to be creative and risk takers, however leadership must also be able to read people and empathize. People will not be inspired if the leader does not understand the perspectives and dreams of team members.

Coaching style

This is the least-used tool in the leader's toolkit. The reason is that it does not always look like leadership. The coaching style involves talking to someone one-on-one, not about the task or the job but about the person. "Who are you? I'd like to get to know you; I'd like to understand you. What do you want in your life? What's your life like? What do you want for your career? What do you want from your job? How can I help you get what you want, go where you want to go?"

The conversation opens up dialogue that lets the leader express the task in ways that make sense to that person. It also creates loyalty and immense commitment to the leader and the team. Unfortunately, many managers are inept at using the coaching style. Too often, they think they're coaching when they're actually micro-managing. Good coaches ask themselves, 'Is this about my issue or theirs?' The difference between leadership and managing is especially evident here.

Affiliative style (Linking and partnering)

The affiliative style creates harmony in the group by getting people to connect with each other. These leaders create a backdrop whereby people can spend time together, get to know each other, and then bond together. The focus is on people and their feelings more than on tasks and goals. Lavish praise is very much a part of this leadership style. The group works more harmoniously together, even under pressure because of the emotional bonding. A negative to this type of leadership is that, with much focus on praise and making people feel good, conflict is not always dealt with and poor performance goes undisciplined. For the best use of this leadership style it should be used in conjunction with another style and used carefully.

Democratic style

The democratic leader listens to others and takes their opinion into consideration when making decisions. It is not about just following the group; that wouldn't be leadership. This style is not suitable for a crisis situation, but when the way forward is not clear, a leader can ask for the team opinions. Perhaps they know more about the situation than the leader does. If a leader can truly listen, people are made to feel more a part of the team; but it can be overused, with endless meetings and never-ending discussions which lack conclusions, except, perhaps, to hold another team meeting.

Pacesetting style

The pacesetter is typically someone who, as an individual, was superb, even outstanding, and so became team leader. Often however, in these situations, the Peter Principle can come into effect. That is: someone is promoted to their highest level of incompetence.

All too often people come into those positions unprepared. The pacesetter leads by [heroic] example and becomes very impatient when people cannot meet the expected standard. Because feedback is generally negative, the emotional climate of the team is low or at the very least, hindered.

If the team is a highly motivated and highly competent one, if team members have been hand-picked and resemble the leader, a really great team may be formed. Regrettably, most teams are not like that. Leaders become impatient when they do not understand the differences in styles and talents.

Commanding style

This is the command-and-control model, a military model. Basically, it is "Do it because I say so! I'm the boss." This might work in an emergency, but in the day-to-day situations it will not work because it ignores how people feel. Typically the leader will bark orders. This type of leadership is rarely used now, but there are still some that operate in this mode. Most likely, it will ultimately create a negative emotional reality.

Leadership with a team has shown that generally a leader will have at least four of the above styles. It was discovered, however, that leaders who have a full repertoire have the best success, both in the business sector and in education. A Hay Group study of headmasters in U.K. schools found that when the head of the school displayed all of these styles, the students had the best academic performance.

Since very few people will have all, or even a few of the styles mentioned above, at times someone or other from the team will step forward to become a leader in a given moment, contributing the particular value that they bring to the common effort. Certainly this will be the case if it is a harmonious team.

ACHIEVING THROUGH THE POWER OF TEAMS

An illustration from one of Aesop's fables probably most clearly defines the power of teams and how leadership must use this strength. A certain man had several sons who were always quarreling with one another, and, try as he might, he could not get them to live together in harmony. So he determined to convince them of their foolishness.

Each one was asked to fetch a bundle of sticks, and in turn they were to break the bundle across their knees. All the sons tried and they all failed. The father then untied a bundle, and handed his sons the sticks one by one. Of course they then had no difficulty at all in breaking them, "There, my boys," he said, "United you will be more than a match for your enemies: but if you quarrel and separate, your weakness will put you at the mercy of those who attack you." Union is strength.

Clearly a fundamental truth of group or team work is taught: even weaker people are powerful when united in a strong team. One of the most effective ways to mobilize and energize people is through teams. Teams are the vehicle to get people involved and contributing.

LEADERSHIP TRUTH:
Teams help ordinary people achieve
extraordinary results.

To be able to move a group from what it is to what it could become as a team *is* effective leadership. Team members and leaders are being challenged to share responsibility for the effectiveness of the team's outcome. When there is broad ownership and participation, the team becomes highly effective and everyone works together to achieve the goals.

Despite the increase of team focus, many groups have not evolved into real teams. Often, teams are left to themselves, unfocused and un-coordinated in their efforts. Questions that might be asked of teams include:

- What is our purpose?
- Do we have a vision? If so, where are we going with it?
- How will we work together, what are our values as a team?
- Who are our partners?
- What is expected of us?
- Do we have gaps that reflect a difference between expectations and our performance?
- What are our goals and priorities?
- Do we have a plan for improvement?
- What skills do we need to develop?
- Is there any outside or other support available?
- How will performance be tracked?

- How/when will we review, assess, celebrate, and refocus?
- Can we individually handle evaluation and correction?

LEADERSHIP TRUTH:
Leadership is not "Me", but "We".

Around each of these questions, teams should develop answers and related action steps. Bringing a team together with a shared focus and taking the action necessary to make it happen is a powerful way to mobilize and energize all of the resources available to an effort. Answers to these questions may also help assessment of newly formed teams and assist the effort to draw them together productively. Additionally, these questions will assist existing teams to refocus and renew themselves, adding or providing needed momentum.

> "In a study by the Center for Creative Leadership of top American and European executives whose careers derailed, the inability to build and lead a team was one of the most common reasons for failure. Team skills, which had been of little consequence in a similar study in the early 1980s, had emerged as a key mark of leadership ten years later. By the 1990s, teamwork became the most frequently valued managerial competence in studies of organizations around the world."[53]

Good managers have always fostered teamwork. If that were not the case, the idea of using a team-based managerial style would have been left by the wayside long ago. However, highly effective leaders are now showing the performance power of building a team-based organization rather than the old style, single-man manager. When effectively organized and led, teams reflect the following advantages. They can:

- Multiply an organization's flexibility and response times.
- Provide a vehicle for wide-scale participation in organizational change and improvement efforts.
- Turn involvement and empowerment expressions into reality.
- Expand jobs and elevate the sense of purpose and meaning they provide.
- Foster a spirit of community, cooperation, and belonging.
- Build the commitment of those people who will ultimately make — or break — any organizational change or improvement effort.
- Harness the improvement energy and ideas of everyone throughout the organization.
- Multiply intellectual power through sharing collective experiences, thus increasing organizational strength.
- Replace command and control discipline with far more powerful and lasting self and peer discipline.

- Improve communications and deepen understanding of change and improvement decisions being made.
- Produce better problem-solving and more thorough decision-making.[54]

The challenge of the change is in the mind of the would-be leaders. Many managers grew up in a command and control era, military style of leadership. As reviewed earlier, this style is typified by a "strong leader" who is a decisive problem-solver and a tough disciplinarian. He (most were men in the past) took control and "made things happen." Teamwork was defined as everyone pulling together and rallying around the leader's goals. All directions came from him.

Many of these values and work ethics are deeply ingrained for those that are in leadership, as well as for the followers and team members. It stands to reason therefore, that many are finding it difficult to transition to effective team development and leadership.

But it can be done, and it is being done. Any team's effectiveness depends largely upon the effectiveness of the leader. And since this is true for this study, a review at what *leadership effectiveness* depends on would serve us well.

- The leader must have a proper level of **self-confidence**. If a leader is insecure, it will be almost impossible to share power and develop others to release assignments that were originally a part of what the leader performed.

If self-worth is predominately drawn from how well others respect, listen to and follow orders, than it will become difficult to empower and develop a strong team.

- A strong team leader knows that his or her job is **not to be the main problem solver**. This focus only continues to send things "up" the chain for answers and weakens delegation. Therefore the team becomes weaker. Strong team leaders make teams that are equipped to solve problems and will support the team in their efforts.

- The effective leader knows that team members are the **leader's partners**. Leaders are to direct and guide teams, but a strong leader also serves the team. This is defined earlier as servant leadership.

- Strong team **leadership skills** are a must. A *Fortune* magazine poll found that being "a team player and team leader" were the most important skills CEOs felt an MBA (Master's in Business Administration) should have.

Interestingly, this is seen as the single biggest factor in confidence levels within teams. Most certainly there is a strong relationship between the skills of facilitating a team discussion, handling conflict, encouraging and capitalizing on diversity, keeping a meeting on track, building a team's effectiveness, etc., and the leader's enthusiasm for teams.

- A leader must still be an **effective manager**. The team should be a good example of team effectiveness, providing a model for and participation in authentic team leadership others.

And finally, despite differences in style, the leaders of great teams share four behavioral traits. The leaders of Great Groups, according to Warren Bennis at the Leader to Leader Institute:[55]

- **Provide direction and meaning.** They remind people of what's important and why their work makes a difference.

- **Generate and sustain trust.** The group's trust in itself and its leadership allows members to accept dissent and ride through the turbulence of the group process.

- **Display a bias toward action, risk taking, and curiosity**. A sense of urgency and a willingness to risk failure to achieve results is at the heart of every great team.

- **Are sources of hope**. Effective team leaders find both tangible and symbolic ways to demonstrate that the group can overcome the odds.

Leadership of a group or team is not a simple matter. Perhaps a good starting point is for leadership to rethink the notion of what teamwork means and how it is achieved, as hopefully we have been doing here. Leadership training and education in the work place needs more than ever to focus on group development as well as individual development.

All great teams, great organizations, families, and groups are built around a shared dream or motivating purpose. It is not enough to punch a time clock or just go to meetings. The mission, the purpose, should reflect with meaning and great significance what the team believes. For leadership, this is a vital part of the job. Whether we appreciate the thought or not, if work is uninspired it is often the failure of the leader. When teams work toward a shared purpose, so much can be accomplished.

Author Luciano de Crescanzo observed that, "We are all angels with only one wing; we can only fly while embracing one another." Ultimately, a leader will know great groups and teams are not really managed, rather they are led in flight.[56]

There has been an explosion of teams and team-based concepts in the organizational fields. But remember: not all teams are a team. Some are groups, clubs, etc. It is necessary for the 21st century leader to understand and implement the real power of *team*. Traditional leadership styles will always be an option, and they will have their times and places. However, in today's global and virtual society, often multiple leadership or team units are required to achieve desired goals. If this is the case, then team discipline or team leadership should be and must be implemented.

What is the difference between single leadership and team leadership? Simply: single-leader leadership is defined by assigning tasks and goals that are best accomplished by individuals who are working within a single leader's direction. Team Leadership is defined as a best practice when tasks and goals require close collaboration among two or more people who are working together, in real time, with access to multiple leaders.

It is time for leaders to quit looking over everyone's shoulders—whether for fear of failure, perceived loss of position, ignorance of today's realities, or simply the inability to conceive of and coordinate team members—and give people the freedom necessary to use their gifts for the sake of the team and for the cause of the vision.

For much more discussion on the topic of teams and leadership interaction, see our companion book, *Building by Team,* as well as the appropriate section in *Beginning to Manage.*

Anyone can steer the ship, but it takes
a leader to chart the course.
- Nehemiah (paraphrased)

Look over your shoulder now and then
to be sure someone's following you.
- Henry Gilmer

Our chief want is someone who will
inspire us to be what we know
we could be
- Ken Blanchard

Chapter Nine
Leaders and Longevity

So much more could and should be addressed in order to give proper attention to the subject of leadership. The absolute need for effective leaders, and not just able bodies, is acute. Leadership studies are blossoming as a field and as an industry for this very reason: leaders are in short supply and large demand! And because leadership is personal and given to specific situations or environments, the components of leadership, the things that *could* be studied and discussed, are really quite endless.

I have endeavored so far in this book to address items that are crucial to effective leadership in this day and age, and more importantly, as we go into the future. They deal more with attitude, perspective and environment than with the traditional tools and techniques common to leadership studies.

Alas, I can not cover all aspects of leadership, its particular needs, its potential and its development. Before we conclude, however, there are a few items left that should be addressed in this discussion of leadership attitudes, perspectives and environment. They include longevity and reproduction through mentoring, dealing with change and opposition, and finally, a commitment to creativity.

LEADERS LIVE ON

I took a note from Brian van Deventer, who is my co-writer in this series of books, and who has led field-based mission programs for the last fifteen years. He has stated that, "No matter what stage of leadership you are in now, it should always be in your thoughts and actions to prepare the next generation of leadership." I agree.

Producing leaders for the next generation should be a top priority on every leader's agenda. How this will be done has much to do with a process that we must take some time to discuss: that of mentoring. Repeatedly through this study we have sought to solidify the understanding that you cannot just send someone to class and expect them to come out a mature leader. Great people and great teams are not built with books, but with continued contact between leaders and followers.

Unfortunately, there is a huge gap between what is communicated and what is actually lived out in leadership today. A lot of people gravitate toward and promote the idea of "passing the torch," of creating next generation leadership. But in the reality of day to day affairs, little (or no) attention is given to making the idea come to life. With true leadership, this will not —can not — be done by shipping a person off to training in some distant place. The classrooms of others cannot be made accountable to prepare your legacy in the people with whom you serve.

You're the only who can accomplish that, and you will accomplish it through mentoring.

To be a master mentor, for those under your leadership now and for the generation of leaders still to come, means to be vulnerable. We need to show others our lives. And the more people we are responsible to lead the more others lay claim to us and, therefore, can restrict us. This is a cost of servant leadership and of mentoring. This personal cost, however, is the gift that will empower others in the team to be successful now and tomorrow.

LEADERSHIP TRUTH:
Mentoring helps us start and finish well!

LEADERS, MENTORS, AND COACHES

There is a price to be paid for the preparation of leaders. Mentoring is a relational experience; meaning that leadership cannot be done effectively from behind the desk. The process can take place in a variety of environments, one-on-one or with teammates. In every scenario there should be conduct that suggests a contract between participants, a contract that says basically, "We are committed to be a team, whether two or more, in a climate of mutual respect and learning." Because leadership rises or falls on how we work together, mentoring of an individual or a team requires open and transparent communication in order to create a healthy environment of communal activity.

As we strive to produce more leaders, to raise up those around us to achieve their greatest potential, mentoring helps the individual to realize that potential through relationship-building and sharing practical applications of values, skills, experiences, problems solved, etc. It is a collaborative process that creates what is often called the "classroom of life," wherein real and intense learning takes place.

It takes time for a mentor to produce such an impact, sometimes a major investment of time. The mentor will set aside time to meet regularly with the person being mentored. Various things will be discussed in those meetings: What is on the mind of the person being mentored? Are there any people issues that are troubling? Are there areas that require personal assistance on the part of the mentor?

Time should be spent also addressing items related to the organization and/or team, the vision of the team, and assignments that are, or are not as the case may be, being followed through. There will be discussion of ways to overcome challenges in fulfilling the personal and career missions of the person being mentored. Complete openness and trust by both parties is not optional; it is vital to the process.

The mentor will demonstrate how he is conducting his own mission, and may ask the student to assist him where appropriate. Thus, through such intimate training, he or she is exhibiting the "how to" through modeling, example and actual implementation. This modeling package is not only about the tasks to be done in the course of a career, but also the lifestyle of the leader. This is why relationship building is so important. While it doesn't replace classroom learning, it is a necessary component of assisting new leaders.

Those who use mentoring often say, rightly so, that it creates more commitment and involvement than other methods of leadership training. And the benefits continue. Once the first group of leaders is ready, having benefited from a masterful mentor, they can in turn use their experience to mentor others into leadership. All of this collaborative mentoring creates hands-on learning that reproduces leaders throughout the organization.

Before proceeding further, some clarity is needed for two words that are often interchangeable in leadership circles: *coaching* and *mentoring*. Both are processes that enlist the cause of hands-on, personal attention of leaders/managers to aid development. Both processes help to enable individuals and corporations to achieve their full potential. In the book *Beginning to Manage*, we lend support to this notion,

> "There are some who would divide the concepts of *mentoring* and *coaching* into two different spheres. And I do concede the point. Coaches are those… who are intimately involved in guiding, assessing and helping indiv-

151

iduals to excel in their given areas...
those of this school of thought will
prefer to identify mentors as outside
forces who may be turned to for
counsel, guidance and, at times, a
kind of therapy, apart from the
immediate work environment. They
are people who are knowledgeable in
the field, and willing to share that
influence and insight with you for the
benefit of your growth and advance."[57]

So, coaching and mentoring share many
similarities but still have distinct potential. The
impact of coaches in the work environment
varies with the work situation. Mentors do
likewise, but often from a greater distance; and
mentors will be more involved in outside life-
interests and concerns of the apprentice. Still,
both coaches and mentors are contributors to
the personal development process of an individual. Leaders are often both, in given times
and situations. Some of the commonalities are:

- Helping the individual make real and lasting
  change by exploring needs, motivations,
  desires, skills and thought processes.
- Supporting the individual in setting
  appropriate goals and methods of assessing
  progress in relation to these goals.
- Observing, listening and asking questions
  designed to bring about understanding.
- Encouraging a commitment to action and
  development for lasting personal growth and
  change.

The mentor is at all times supportive and non-judgmental of views, lifestyle and aspirations. I say non-judgmental because there is a difference between judgment and constructive criticism. In this relationship, the trust and openness that is required calls for inviting attitudes. Criticism and differing points of views should be shared, but always offered in the right attitude.

It is also important to address the issue of dependency. The mentor must always work to ensure that individual abilities are developed, rather than fostering unhealthy dependencies on the coaching or mentoring relationship. Children are raised to leave home, and apprentices are raised to go out and prosper. Such crucial issues require the mentor to evaluate the outcomes of the process, using objective measures wherever possible, to ensure the relationship is successful and the individual is achieving their personal goals.

This is just a brief look at coaching and mentoring, tools that no organization or group can overlook in as much as an organization's most valuable resource is its people. Coaching and mentoring can be used to effectively unlock the knowledge and passion within the hearts and minds of people. This potential exists wherever there are people, and organizations and groups cannot afford to overlook this wealth of potential. (See more on this subject in our book, *Start Right, Finish Strong: A guide to coaching and mentoring*, or in chapter three, "Managing People", of *Beginning to Manage*.)

LEADERS ARE CHANGE AGENTS

Change is always difficult. It is one of the most problematic issues for leadership, whether in the home or at the office. I introduce this topic briefly at this point because the leader who learns to mentor/coach will always have the opportunity to instill awareness and receptivity to inevitable change. Every leader-in-development and every established mentor is destined to deal with change. It is a critical concern, for nothing can be more hazardous to leadership health than unexpected or unprepared change. And no tool in the box should be handled more carefully then the change that a leader might inspire.

Imagine the scenario: you have accepted a new position and the first thing that you're told is that you will not be allowed to make any changes. But how can that be? "If you never move the vase, a permanent stain will be left on the table!" It is a must to learn how to avoid situations where you cannot make any change. Your predecessor might have been exceedingly successful, but without the ability to initiate change you will never be able to leave an imprint or lead the group.

> ### LEADERSHIP TRUTH:
> ### Leaders are the chief pioneers for the change process.

Six famous last words are, "We've always done it that way!" Why change? When an organization begins to drift or lose passion, change is often the key. If the group becomes ineffective or there are patterns of repeated failure, *it is* time to change.

Life is an example: Our bodies change; it's an unstoppable process. A mentor provides an invaluable service when reminding us that, just as you cannot stop aging, you cannot stop progress. The individual or leader who is not open to change will be useless. The impact of Generation X and the changing face of global economics have brought new demands on every front. Change is inevitable, and relevance requires that we deal with it!

The list can go on to illustrate that change is necessary, and it can be like facing a mountainous challenge. Leaders are often the ones most concerned about doing something about issues that arise or problems foreseen. Followers may see them, but they often will wait for the leader to take the risk to bring about the change. He must be willing and prepared to be that instrument.

Futurist Alvin Toffler observes, "The illiterate of the 21st century will not be those who cannot read and write, but those who cannot learn, unlearn, and relearn." Each generation has its own values and culture based on life during their formative years. If I compare the world today to what it was when I was a teenager, it is as though I lived on a different planet; it was a much different time and a much different place.

We must come to understand that change is inevitable.

Servant leaders, mentors and coaches must definitely become valuable instigators and handlers of constantly changing climates. There is a lot of material available in leadership and management training today to address this challenge. The excellent leader would do well to acquire and digest some of that material. An inability to navigate change will, undeniably and unavoidably, render a leader irrelevant. An attitude of resistance or the hope of avoidance simply will not do. Mark it down: the leader who will not cultivate an atmosphere of change, personally and internally, as well as corporately and outwardly, is done.

A LEADER HANDLES OPPOSITION

I once read that Abraham Lincoln had the right idea of criticism; he ignored it.

> "If I were to read, much less answer, all the attacks made on me, this shop might as well be closed for any other business. I do the very best I know how, the very best I can; and I mean to keep doing so until the end. If the end brings me out all right, what is said against me won't amount to anything. If the end brings me out wrong, 10,000 angels swearing I was right would make no difference."[58]

Generally, it seems that when things go well, they go really well; people are on board. But, when things go badly, it is all down hill from there. People are soon in flight. How should a leader handle criticism and conflict? It is a painful thing to be criticized. It can debilitate. Yet everyone in leadership, whether at the office, home or at the club, *will* face criticism and opposition at some time. Change that: many times.

Unfortunately, it is often an ironic truth that the more effective you are and the more mature you become, the more criticism and attacks you will face. Certainly if there is an increase in the number of followers, it stands to reason that the attack will be greater simply in response to the greater number of those available to voice criticism. Most major governments and corporations have offices that operate just to react to such situations.

Leaders will be misunderstood and often attacked; the next day may often accompany the desire to run away. The key is to distinguish between the genuine desire to quit and the feeling of the moment that surely another group of people and circumstances would be preferable. Often as leaders, we do not desire to abandon our roles; we simply want the benefactors of our leadership to soften up, smarten up or go away. True leaders will overcome rejection for the good of the role.

There are many reasons why leaders are at times found under fire, attacked and criticized. The reasons are as varied as the circumstances of leadership, but most of the conflicts can probably be attributed to the differences in people, their nature and, ultimately, selfishness. A brief look at a few main reasons for attack and criticism can help bring perspective. Sometimes attacks are justified (could it be?) but it may be simply a matter of individual feelings of loss; something has not been provided that was desired, someone's needs were not met. Consider these:

- Jealousy
- Unfulfilled expectations
- Misunderstandings
- Accurate criticisms
- Organizational crisis
- Values conflict
- Failure
- Distrust
- Pride and arrogance

When a leader is criticized, the response can often be negative. But maturity speaks when a leader faces criticism with a positive view. Criticism can actually become a process that can aid personal leadership development. Although extremely difficult to do in the moment, certainly there is something that can eventually be learned. Even if only two percent of the criticism was correct, the ability to recognize that we all have blind spots that need correcting will be a positive response and will produce good results.

When criticism comes, what do you do? Some of the greatest, suggested reactions are:

- Keep silent
- Think before you react or speak
- Really listen
- Respond gently
- Agree with whatever is true
- Give feedback with care
- Avoid quarreling
- Offer to help
- Ask for forgiveness.[59]

Or, to quote a modern day proverb: "If life hands you lemons, make lemonade." Be aware, too, that handling conflict is not only about attacks received personally against your own leadership. There will be times when those under your guidance will fight with one another. When two or more team members cannot stop fighting, what do you do? When your wisdom has been exhausted, where do you turn? How might you turn this situation positive?

The book, *Practical Supervision,* offers some great guidelines toward this end.[60]

- Mediate rather than judge
- Give it time [but don't let it fester)
- Don't accuse or lay blame
- Go back to basics

- Win admissions – and forgiveness – of mistakes
- Find grounds for cooperation

Followers will always have occasion to be skeptical of each other and of leadership. A leader can work and strive to gain favor and respect, and to engender that in the community, but unfortunately there will always be certain faults that irritate others and you. Making room for valid criticisms and feedback will do much to aid matters. Creating positive outlets for this kind of behavior will serve much better than keeping things closed up, bottled and potentially explosive. The more open and transparent communication is engendered, the greater is the possibility of keeping cancerous criticism away from your leadership and keeping it away from your team mates.

Remember: don't forget to listen to what people tell you about your leadership. Follow the 80/20 rule of success: eighty percent of the time we will get it right, and 20 percent of the time we will blow it. When the 20 percent times come, listen. It might only be 2 percent that is valid, but there is such a potential for growth in that 2 percent.

A LEADER EXERCISES CREATIVITY

Life is in a constant state of development. A leader cannot afford to fall behind. But, neither is it a matter of being frantic to keep up with each and every new thought, innovation, news item and latest craze. Flexibility is important, but not everything can be explored. The wisdom to choose pursuits is so very necessary.

The real danger is paralysis. After we have done something for a number of years in a certain way, we naturally think we are experts [especially if that activity has been even moderately successful]. But time can generate a certain isolation and conformity to tradition. Comfort zones are called that for a reason; they're comfortable!

Being creative and cultivating creativity will force us to look at the world with new eyes that are wide open. Creativity will cause a leader to question the way things are being done and constantly look for improvement. Great leaders are always exploring options, looking for ways to improve.

The Japanese have a great word for this pursuit, *kaizen*. It is the ability to make small improvements everyday in our processes and products. Giant leaps are important, but moderate, consistent steps make the real impact. In Japan, every worker is expected to find some way each day to get just one-tenth of 1 percent improvement in what he does or makes.[61]

It is commonly said that old age is a matter of mind, when you stop learning you become old. A key to great leadership is to utterly embrace an ongoing learning process. At the heart of

161

creativity is the ability to come up with fresh new approaches to difficult situations and improvements to the routine and mundane. The prospect of trying new things and moving away from the tried and true might be intimidating, but the rewards are limitless.

One way to nurture creativity when you face a problem is to make a list of possible solutions, no matter how crazy they may seem. Work your way down that list until you come up with something that will work for you. That's a creative process and involves the willingness to think, to examine, and to try something new.

It takes time to be creative. Impatience can often derail the process, because the first solution is not necessarily the best. The busyness of life is an enemy of patience and creativity. When we stop and ask others for input and explore new materials and examine the possibilities, then we have enhanced our creative abilities.

There is good news: creativity is not the domain of youth alone. This is the day of honoring and recognizing creativity and entrepreneurship at every age. We're living longer, producing better and experiencing opportunities that have never been available in times past. Age is only a discriminator when we allow it to be, and there is a lot of creative product yet to be released from some of us who are no longer the up-and-comers. Creativity is a matter of the spirit and

the mind, not the body clock. Commit yourself,
whatever your age, to be bold, risky and creative!

w. turned world upside-down.
God is my source of strength.

Ref. (Pg. 148)

Reading this fragment made me think of the fact
that the disciples of Jesus turned the world
"upside down". What made them succeed was not
their education, cause most of them didn't have
any, but it is the contact they had with the
Master Teacher while on earth, and the relationship
they had with him after He left earth.

1. If we were the original disciples of Jesus,
would we change anything from the way we
do things today?
—Because we are the disc. of Jesus today and
He is our Master which is the same yest.
tod. + forever. He ideal would have us
to bring the world upside down from Jesus now.
Since we are not where we ought to be than we
need more passion + commitment in doing His work,
what we need to change is the relationship +
closeness we have with the Lord. We need to be
in close contacts with Jesus, like the early disc. were.

2. Since Being a Leader a mentor who prepares the
next gen. can be tiring and draining. How
can leaders avoid to burn out?
We can do nothing on our own strength. Anytime
I've tried I've failed. Our source of strength is
God to him we should turn to review, refresh
us + comfort us. Spiritual leaders cannot afford
to stay away from their Father!

If the blind lead the blind, both shall fall in the ditch.
- *Jesus of Nazareth*

The task of the leader is to get his people from where they are to where they have not been.
- *Henry Kissinger*

The final test of a leader is that he leaves behind him in other men, the conviction and the will to carry on.
- *Walter Lippmann*

Chapter Ten
A Legacy through Succession

One of the most important reasons that you, as a leader, are to be preparing next-generation leaders through personal coaching and mentoring is that you are aware that you will not be around forever. One of the most overlooked and underappreciated aspects of excellent leadership—no matter what lip service we give to it—is that of succession that is accomplished purposefully and fruitfully. I am going to address it at some length for two reasons: first, because I believe it is an essential element of good leadership and secondly because I want to be committed to the premise in my own conduct. Much of the legacy that we can pass on will rest on this important issue.

LEADERSHIP TRUTH:
Real succession management is a
key to long-term success.

It would be fair to say that most organizations recognize the benefit of having a highly functional system for passing the leadership mantle. But, the task of preparing and planning for a presently serving leader to exit is often put off for another time in the future. For example, even after knowing in April 2005 that Peter Jennings, the talented anchorman of ABC's

World News Tonight, was suffering from inoperable lung cancer, the program did not identify a long-term successor, perhaps to avoid seeming insensitive. However, to have had a succession plan in place would have allowed Mr. Jennings to not only to have a say in the selection process, but to mentor the replacement to step into his highly demanding and prestigious role. His imprint would have been that much greater.

Sometimes leaders and organizations leave the idea of succession alone because to identify any successors might cause other talented, appreciated people to move on. Not having been identified as next in line, they might choose to find other, seemingly more hopeful ground. Yet, as I look and ask around, it seems rarely to be the fact, and most who have practiced solid programs of succession would say that those they have lost were probably on the way out anyway. Loyalty is appreciated by loyal people, even when it is expressed fundamentally toward someone else. Somewhere in the mind is retained the fact that, if loyalty is proved toward one (the chosen successor at the appropriate time), then come their day, it will be there for them too.

Significant *plans*, at least, for long term succession must be demonstrated. They must be in place not only for top level management but for the entire spectrum of positions. If there are plans for only one or two senior positions to be replaced, many problems can

166

arise. Programs of succession should be a fundamental part of the corporate fabric where you are leading. A holistic and strategic approach to succession management aids in building the internal talent strength. Planning should focus on compiling a list of possible replacements that would identify and develop high-potential leaders who demonstrate the ability to execute the strategy of the organization.

LEADERS MAKE SUCCESSION PLANS

What are the cornerstones for a good succession plan? It hinges on having a strategic, systematic, and consistent approach that develops future employee and organizational capability. This can range from simple replacement planning to integrated development planning. I like the thoughts given by Robert Gandossy and Nidhi Verma in their work, "Passing the Torch of Leadership," so I will summarize for you here. In it, they maintain that the core process of developing a reliable channel of successors depends on five cornerstones: *Alignment, Commitment, Assessment, Development, and Measurement.*[62]

Keep in mind as you begin to explore this, however, that a plan is only as good as its execution. In order for there to be success in the plan, without question, there must be an unwavering commitment to enact it. No matter how carefully designed a strategy is, it remains a useless strategy until you give it life. So now let's begin to unpack and add some details to these identified succession cornerstones.

Alignment

Companies and organizations need to strive constantly to build a reliable supply of talent. This is not only to fill vacancies but to achieve future vision and long term strategies. The alignment principle is defined as reflecting the attitudes and behaviors of the organization. As a leader, you are looking for good people to become a part of your experience.

In 2005, IBM refreshed the leadership com- petencies it had developed in 2003 to reflect the rapidly changing environment. Desiring to be more future-focused; the company's approach became, "On-demand leadership for an on- demand world." Thirty senior leaders were interviewed who embodied what IBM believed it needed for future success. A new leadership model was developed that comprised com- petencies required by IBM's leaders to build an "on-demand" culture, which has been identified as a very successful transition. They identified the people, and build the process around them.

Commitment

Leaders must take an active role in the succession management process. It should be promoted and led by example. At General Electric, former CEO Jack Welch, and now Jeff

Immelt, made leadership development a top priority and have demanded that executives follow suit. As a result, GE promotes nearly 85 percent of its leaders from within. At one top company the CEO maintains a mentoring partnership program wherein he meets with early and mid-career high-potentials throughout the year.

Secondly, it should be a strict discipline of leaders to hold managers accountable for identifying and developing talent in their work are. This can be done by tying it to their reward or promotion.

Finally, through steps of investment in financial and people resources for succession management, the point will be reinforced that senior leadership believes in the importance of succession management. It will become part of the organization.

Identification

Jobs and positions that are vital for the long-term performance and health of the organization must be identified. Also, individuals that can fill these positions with competency are critical components of a succession management process. Based on the organization's strategic plans, successors are to be assessed: their attitudes, skills and competencies. After identifying candidates, classification of their readiness is evaluated. As positions open, the selection will be much more suitable.

Identification promotes a consistent talent review process. It will impede selection of a candidate based on personal and often limited impressions of the individual. This process must not be limited to upper level positions only.

Development

Adopting development strategies is a priority for the most successful companies. Future leaders will be developed through specific experiences to enhance their capabilities for their 'destination jobs.' This will mean in some cases internal leaders developed by moving them within countries, within regions, and around the world.

Proctor and Gamble believes people need to be in a role for three to five years to be assessed and developed. "We want people in roles for three to five years so they live with their own mess," says Moheet Nagrath, Proctor and Gamble's vice president of Human Resources Global Operations.

Home Depot works to develop an employee's career at every step, offering structured assessment and development programs to ensure that talent is recognized and developed. The participants in these programs enter a series of rotational leadership programs: store leadership, merchandising, business leadership, and internal audit roles. There are no pro- motions at Home Depot without an objective assessment. At times throughout the year, high potential employees have the benefit of world-renowned educators who are invited to facilitate intensive leadership development programs.

Intel practices a method called "two in a box." It places high priority on grooming internal talent. The "two in a box" method allows executives to overlap job duties, each one both teaching and learning in the relationship.

Organizations may jeopardize success of their development programs by:

- Adopting a one-size-fits-all training approach.
- Omitting accountability for managing and monitoring programs.
- Endorsing a polarized approach where management does not work together to develop employees.

Measurement

Measuring the victories and learning from the failures of a succession management program is a must. Measurement helps assess the effectiveness of the overall program and works to track the success of an individual placement.

Since measurement of a succession initiative is subjective at best, many companies do not even bother to establish a system whereby measuring is possible. When an organization does not implement measurement, it runs the risk of making process for leadership succession outdated and out of touch with real business and individual succession needs. The system of measurement must be custom fit to the needs and expectations of the organization. Management programs that are models for succession use a variety of measures to ensure that desired outcomes are achieved. Targets are set to ensure continuous improvement. These include:

- How leadership openings can be filled from internal pools.
- How many qualified candidates per leadership position are available.
- Considering ethnic and gender diversity in promotions.
- Knowing how many positions have two or more "ready now" candidates.
- Percentage of high-potentials who complete development plans.
- Attrition rate from the succession pool.

Great performance is not just about reaching the top; it is also about staying there. Tracking and measuring the progress and development of individuals targeted for succession is very important. If an organization fails to review and measure those with high-potential at regular intervals, it may be discovered that top talent is underachieving, and therefore no longer a high potential consideration.

LEADERS EXECUTE SUCCESSION PLANS

Typically, problems in the execution of succession plans derive from a combination of process issues and people issues. In some ways, we have addressed these concerns at intervals throughout the book. To summarize, however, keep in mind that:

- Process-based problems come from vague and makeshift succession management strategies. Generally succession management tools are difficult to understand and the roles and responsibilities of new leadership are not clear; in the process of implementation, frequent changes are made to the original process, making it ultimately impotent.

- People-issues often develop from the reluctance of managers and employees to commit the necessary time and resources to addressing the process; further, personal insecurities and prejudices in current leadership can compound the difficulty in selecting top talent.

Organizations and companies that have effective and enduring succession management programs pay attention to and iron out process and people-related problems. Hewitt Associates, a leading human resource firm, has reported that at present the top twenty companies integrate these competencies 100 percent into the succession planning process, while only 78 percent of other companies do so. They perform, and they perform well.

Leaders who refuse to initiate, much less be a part of, succession programs, are simply refusing to respond to the lessons of reality. Organizations that plan are led by people who plan. Such groups succeed, and such leaders succeed.

LEADERS INVEST IN THE FUTURE

No company, organization, charity, no management program can safeguard itself against key talent departures. At some point critical positions become vacant, through retirement, resignation, poor performance, or untimely death. The organization is forced to search for a replacement. If the group has not invested in building its future leadership internally, this search can pose significant operational and financial risk

Certainly for leadership development there are long term benefits if a succession process is in place. The cornerstones described in this chapter are simple but often overlooked. Through planning, performing, and succeeding in the five succession management cornerstones, we can develop a reservoir of competent successors for our targeted, mission-critical positions.

ON A PERSONAL NOTE

We see that the conception and implementation of plans for those who come after us are important. But the material can seem awfully impersonal, as though it relates to those who are "out there", but somehow is not so relevant "right here". The examples offered are of large corporations, influential people working in key sectors with enormous staffs and huge payrolls.

But do not misunderstand. The reason that such attitudes and thought processes are used in the large forums is simple: they work. Sometimes we think that the rules are different for those who function at different levels of the game. But hear me: successful leadership is successful leadership. The rules apply across the board.

If you are in leadership, you need to be aware, I think, that you are really only as effective as the generations that come after you. You are a building block, not the end of the process. Those who follow should be able to build on the strength you have left behind.

I've worked too long and hard to believe that my contributions will end with me. My desire is that our lifetime accomplishments will leave an indelible imprint. That is not to say that everything we are and do is a good example, but society is full of forces that try to mold every part of our lives. Why shouldn't my life and yours be just as powerful in shaping those who come after us? Leadership should be nurturing, as families are, to help those we lead to find and fulfill their great life-shaping desires. It is inconceivable that I, or we, should lead and leave no challenge for those following to rise to the next level after we step off the leadership stage.

We need to imagine that our lives today will identify with new lives tomorrow. That can be one of the most deeply exciting things to help us shape the manner in which we live until the end. This is beyond formulas and corporate manuals; it's personal. Maybe we won't have recognition in the eyes of other people, but in the eyes of those we impact, there is that recognition and challenge, to carry our imprint to the next level of excellence.

Our common concern is excellence in leadership: today *in me*. Excellence in leadership: tomorrow *in others*, especially those my life impacts.

Let it be so!

VV. "You will be my disciples ... "

Ref.
If we fail in preparing the next generation for leadership, we are ~~risking~~ doomed to failure. The Bible clearly says that: "If you don't worship, the stones will" The work of the Lord will still be completed, He will find a way, we just would fail ~~having~~ being a part of that blessing.

1. If Christ was to come tom. would there be recognition in his eyes for my work?

Dread Question...

2. Excellent leadership, to be measured by his or our terms? How so?

176

3. We ~~see~~ recognise Jesus is our example in everything

Concluding Thought

Finishing well is my goal. I ask myself sometimes what my family and friends will remember
about me. Certainly this will be colored by how I
cope with transition of leadership. Many who
have been successful all along the rest of the
journey will fail in this one point. Rules you
make, those you live by, must be couched in
grace. Someone gave grace to you to enable
leadership to be born out in your life. Give grace
to every age. It is the little things that so often
trip us up. When it is time to pass the torch,
recognize it with grace and willingly transition to
the next leader and the next generation,
confident of the fact that you have birthed into
them great leadership skill.

- Did he plan for the future in order for us to do so?

Afterword

It serves us well to note that, from beginning to end, our approach to management and all of its related fields is buttressed by a simple truth: we are informed by our faith. Throughout the text, we have endeavored to expound principles which are in line with our under-standing of Christian life and conduct. We trust that this would not be off-putting to you! We have made no effort to preach to you, and there is no appeal to conversion in these pages, as you have seen. We do contend, however, that the Christian life and ethic actually coincide with the best of management principles. The morality and instruction that is provided in a thorough understanding of the Christian faith is not only helpful, but embellishing of the best characteristics of a good manager.

Should you desire to know more of our perspectives on this matter, and the manner in which it can inform your personal life, your work place and the lives of others, please do not hesitate to contact us. We are available to you.

Contact:

EME
PO Box 73004
Ano Glyfada 16510
Greece

Tel. +30 210 9651346   Fax. +30 210 9644920
ememin@hol.gr

Appendix One:
Leadership Self Test

Are You A Leader? Part I: The Leadership Self Test

As today's organizations become more and more lean, people in business are gaining a greater appreciation for the differences between a manager's style of thinking and a leader's style of thinking.

When people like Frederick Taylor first began to study management, he used a stopwatch to see how well people on a factory floor could improve their productivity. Back then, productivity in the American workforce was determined more by the performance mechanical tasks than by the ability to process information or build service relationships, the way it is today. The purpose of a manager, in Taylor's day, was to be the one who knew the most about the work, and the one who took greater control to assure productivity and profit. Imagine being supervised by a manager with a stopwatch!

Now we live in an information age and no one can "know everything" about a job the way the managers of yesteryear (supposedly) did. In an information age, managers have had to shift toward becoming the ones who create the environment that helps empowered, knowledgeable people to succeed. What's more, the transition to a service economy has placed less of an emphasis on controlling others and more of an emphasis on the human skills of building strong relationships.

As a result, the role of management in the American workforce has shifted, and today's managers, more and more, have to develop leadership skills. Leadership talent is even more essential to success on an executive level.

If you're curious about how much you think like a leader versus thinking like a manager, answer the following fifteen True or False questions. Then follow through to the next section to see the answers and a brief discussion of each question. Formulate your own before moving to the answer section!

LEADERSHIP SELF TEST

1. **TRUE or FALSE:** I think more about immediate results than I do about mentoring others.

2. **TRUE or FALSE:** People will be motivated if you pay them enough.

3. **TRUE or FALSE:** It's nice to know about people's long-term goals, but not necessary to get the job done.

4. **TRUE or FALSE:** If you have a consistent recognition system that rewards everyone in the same way, then that is enough.

5. **TRUE or FALSE:** The best way to build a team is to set a group goal that is highly challenging, maybe even "crazy."

6. **TRUE or FALSE:** My greatest pleasure in my job comes from making the work process more effective.

7. **TRUE or FALSE:** I spend more of my time and attention on my weaker performers than I do on my top performers, who basically take care of themselves.

8. **TRUE or FALSE:** It's better not to know anything about the personal lives and interests of the people who report to me.

9. **TRUE or FALSE:** Sometimes, it's almost as if I'm a "collector of people" because I'm always recruiting and getting to know new people.

10. **TRUE or FALSE:** I like to surround myself with people who are better at what they do than I am.

11. **TRUE or FALSE:** I am a lifelong student of what makes other people tick.

12. **TRUE or FALSE:** People talk about "mission" too much – it's best just to let people do their work and not try to bring values into the conversation.

13. **TRUE or FALSE:** It's my job to know everything that goes on in my area.

14. **TRUE or FALSE:** I pay close attention to how and where I spend my time, because the priorities I put into action are the ones that other people will observe and follow.

15. **TRUE or FALSE:** I've worked hard to get along with or understand people who are very different from me.

This little "Self Test" is meant to provoke thought, and there are no standards here for how many "leader" responses would make you a "true leader."

The answers and ideas offered come from experience with assessments involving hundreds of leaders and managers over time, but this is not a standardized test. I hope you find the discussion below interesting and educational.

Remember, most managerial jobs require some leadership practice, and executives need both strong management and leadership skills. The idea that real people are either "leaders" or "managers" is false - different jobs require a different balance of each.

SELF TEST ANSWERS AND DISCUSSION

1. **TRUE or FALSE: I think more about immediate results than I do about mentoring others.**

Managers focus on the process and immediate efficiency more than leaders do. Leaders think about how they invest their time to develop the strongest talent so that those people can grow and do more and more over time. Leaders figure if they do that, those people will do a better job of watching and improving processes than they themselves will. "True" is more of a manager's response, and "False" is more of a leader's response.

2. **TRUE or FALSE: People will be motivated if you pay them enough.**

Leaders understand that pay is a satisfier, not a true motivator. Once the satisfier is in place at an acceptable level, people are motivated by the nature of the work and challenges, opportunities to learn and grow, and based on whether or not they feel their bosses support or care about them. "True" is more of a manager's answer, and "False" is more of a leader's answer.

3. **TRUE or FALSE: It's nice to know about people's long-term goals, but not necessary to get the job done.**

Someone once said that managers get "work done through people," but leaders get "people

185

done through work." Since leaders need to know what makes individual people tick, they want to know long-term goals and aspirations, so they can craft ways to combine personal goals with the work at hand, or even the organization's goals. For a given project, it may be less important to know people's long-term goals, but for organizational success and growth, it is necessary. "True" is more of a manager's answer, and "False" is more of a leader's answer.

4. **TRUE or FALSE: If you have a consistent recognition system that rewards everyone in the same way, then that is enough.**

Leaders' recognize that everyone is motivated a little differently, and so consistency is not an absolute virtue in recognizing people. Some people may like public praise, and others may emphasize more the opportunity to have flexible family time, for example. Since managers emphasize systems more than they do people or personalities, "True" is more of a manager's response, and "False" is more of a leader's response.

5. **TRUE or FALSE: The best way to build a team is to set a group goal that is highly challenging, maybe even "crazy."**

Manager's tend to think more in terms of what has been done before and try to make more incremental improvements, while leaders like to challenge people to bring out their best in ways they themselves may not have imagined possible. The best way to build team coherence is to take people through a shared, difficult challenge – something any military platoon leader can tell you. "True" is more of a leader's response, and "False" is more of a manager's response.

6. **TRUE or FALSE: My greatest pleasure in my job comes from making the work process more effective.**

This is a classic manager's priority, deriving most pleasure from process and efficiency. Leaders enjoy that a lot too, but they tend to enjoy most when they can help people and organizations grow. "True" is more of a manager's response, and "False" is more of a leader's response.

7. **TRUE or FALSE: I spend more of my time and attention on my weaker performers than I do on my top performers, who basically take care of themselves.**

Leaders use their time as a reward and seek to invest their attention where it can have the most upside impact. Generally speaking, people have the most opportunity to grow and become truly great where they already demonstrate strong performance, and so leaders tend to avoid remedial projects or the constant oversight of weaker performers. Instead, they spend more of their attention on the people who are the best at what they do, since those are the people who will invent the greatest process and performance improvements in the future. Managers tend to focus more on problems to solve than they do on opportunities to boost people toward previously unachieved levels of excellence. "True" is more of a manager's response, and "False" is more of a leader's response.

8. **TRUE or FALSE: It's better not to know anything about the personal lives and interests of the people who report to me.**

Leaders try to learn what makes each person tick, so that means knowing getting to understand them in a more personal way, without being invasive or inappropriate. Managers tend to be more cut-and-dried in their work relations. "True" is more of a manager's response, while "False" is more of a leader's response.

9. **TRUE or FALSE: Sometimes, it's almost as if I'm a "collector of people" because I'm always recruiting and getting to know new people.**

Some of the best managers are very good at studying best practices – ways to "build a better mousetrap" to improve performance and efficiency. Leaders tend to look more for the "Einsteins" and star performers of the world who are more likely to invent those better mousetraps in the first place. Leaders think about people and their talents as if they were investment opportunities, and so "True" is more of a leader's response, and "False" is more of a manager's response.

10. **TRUE or FALSE: I like to surround myself with people who are better at what they do than I am.**

This is a classic leadership statement, since leaders are all about finding and cultivating talent, and are not threatened by it. Managers may tend to want to feel more in control of their surroundings – not least of all because highly talented people can be very independent and difficult to "manage!" Since leaders tend to have stronger social skills than managers do, and so are better prepared to deal with other strong egos, "True" is more of a leader's response, and "False" is more of a manager's response.

11. **TRUE or FALSE: I am a lifelong student of what makes other people tick.**

"True" is more of a leader's response, and "False" is more of a manager's response, for reasons already discussed.

12. **TRUE or FALSE: People talk about "mission" too much – it's best just to let people do their work and not try to bring values into the conversation.**

While it's true that "mission" and "vision" are concepts that have become watered down by careless misuse, leaders still understand that it is best to connect daily work and projects into a larger framework that gives work a sense of purpose and meaning. People would rather feel that their work has some purpose and meaning in order to do their work well and care about results. "True" is more of a manager's response, and "False" is more a leader's response.

13. **TRUE or FALSE: It's my job to know everything that goes on in my area.**

Since leaders focus more on knowing the people who know what is going on, rather than on the details of everything that is going on, "True" is more of a manager's response, and "False" is more of a leader's response.

14. **TRUE or FALSE: I pay close attention to how and where I spend my time, because the priorities I put into action are the ones that other people will observe and follow.**

Leaders realize that the little things they do ripple out in wider and wider ways, and that their actual priorities will be mimicked throughout an organization. As a result, they make their choices wisely, knowing that people, and other managers or supervisors, do imitate the "boss," who sets the ultimate tone. "True" is more of a leader's response, and "false" is more of a manager's response.

15. **TRUE or FALSE: I've worked hard to get along with or understand people who are very different from me.**

As headstrong as many leaders can be, they know from experience that being so headstrong can be a liability, and they have learned to work hard at accepting and listening to other points of view. Managers may be more focused on what they believe to be the "right way" to do some job or work process, and may be less open to widely divergent views. Leaders may not always enjoy hearing other views, but they often have learned the critical importance of the saying, "Let the best idea win!" "True" is more of a leader's response, and "False" is more of a manager's response.

Appendix Two:
Suggested Reading List

The Leadership Trust® recommends the following resources to assist you on your path to leadership excellence and self-awareness. These books are designed to support your professional and personal growth, the latter to include your family, spiritual, private, and social life.

A Better Idea.	Donald Peterson
Acts of Faith	Ivanla Vanzant
Anatomy of the Spirit: The 7 Stages of Power and Healing	Carolyn Myss
Awakening Intuition: Using Your Mind-Body Network for Insight & Healing	Mona Lisa Schultz, MD, PhD
Black Holes and Energy Pirates: How to Recognize and Release Them	Jesse Reeder
Born to Win: Transactional Analysis with Gestalt Experiments	Muriel James & Dorothy Jongeward
Built to Last: Successful Habits of Visionary Companies	James C. Collins & Jerry I.Porras
Celebrate Yourself	Dorothy Corkille Briggs
Conversations With God	Neale Walsch
Developing the Leader Within You	John C. Maxwell
Discover What You're Best At: A Complete Career System	Linda Gale
Do Less, Achieve More	Chin-Ning Chu

Eat to Live	Joel Fuhrman, M.D. & Mehmet Oz
Emotional Intelligence	Daniel Goleman
Energy Anatomy	Caroline Myss
Eyewitness to Power: The Essence of Leadership, Nixon to Clinton	David R. Gergen
Feel the Fear and Do It Anyway	Susan Jeffers
Forbes' Greatest Business Stories of All Time	Daniel Gross
Getting the Love You Want	Harville Hendrix, PhD
Good to Great: Why some Companies Make the Leap and Others Don't	Jim Collins
Handbook to Higher Consciousness	Ken Keyes
Heal Your Body: The Mental Causes for Physical Illness and the Metaphysical Ways to Overcome Them	Louise Hay
Healing the Shame That Binds You	John Bradshaw
How to Meditate	Lawrence Le Shan
How We Choose to be Happy	Rick Foster & Greg Hicks
If Success is a Game, These are the Rules: Ten Rules for a Fulfilling Career and Life	Cherie Carter-Scott, PhD
In Search of Excellence: Lessons From America's Best Run Companies	Thomas J. Peters & Robert H. Waterman
Jonathan Livingston Seagull: A Story	Richard Bach
King, Warrior, Magician, Lover	Robert Moore
Leadership	Rudolph W. Giuliani

Leadership and Spirit: Breathing New Vitality and Energy into Individuals and Organizations	Russ S. Moxley
Leadership the Eleanor Roosevelt Way	Robin Gerber
Leading Change	John P. Kotter
Leading the Way: Three Truths From the Top Companies for Leaders	Robert Gandossy & Marc Effron
Life Strategies: Doing What Works, Doing What Matters	Phillip C. McGraw
Living the Wonder of It All	Ralph S. Marston, Jr
Living Your Best Life: Ten Strategies for Getting From Where You Are to Where You're Meant to Be	Laura Berman Fortgang
Love and Profit: The Art of Caring Leadership	James A. Autry
Love is Letting Go of Fear	Gerald G. Jampolsky
Now, Discover Your Strengths: How to Develop Your Talents and Those of the People You Manage	Marcus Buckingham & Donald O. Clifton
Please Understand Me	David Keirsey & Marilyn Bates
Power of Full Engagement	Jim Loehr & Tony Schwartz
Predictive Parenting	Shad Helmstetter
Primal Leadership: Realizing the Power of Emotional Intelligence	Daniel Goleman, Richard E. Boyatzis & Annie McKee
Principle-Centered Leadership	Stephcn R. Covey
Real Love: The Truth About Finding Unconditional Love & Fulfilling Relationships	Greg S. Baer
Scripts People Live: Transactional Analysis of Life	Claude Steiner

Self Matters: Creating Your Life From the Inside Out	Phillip C. McGraw
Selling the Invisible: Biz Books to Go	Harry Beckwith
Servant Leader	Ken Blanchard
Strategy of the Dolphin: Scoring a Win in a Chaotic World	Dudley Lynch & Paul S. Kordis
Supraconscious Leadership	Joseph Jaworski
Taming Your Gremlin: A Guide to Enjoying Yourself	Richard D. Carson
The 9 Insights of the Wealthy Soul	Michael R. Norwood
The 21 Irrefutable Laws of Leadership	John C. Maxwell
The Act of Happiness	Dalai Lama
The Adventure of Self Discovery	Stanislav Grof
The Art of Possibility: Transforming Professional & Personal Life	Rosamund Stone & Benjamin Zander
The Courage to Create	Rollo May
The Courage to Heal	Ellen Bass
The Daily Motivator To Go	Ralph S Marston, Jr
The Dance of Anger	Harriet Lerner
The Dance of Intimacy	Harriet Lerner
The Experience of Insight	Joseph Goldstein
The Four Agreements: A Practical Guide to Personal Freedom	Don Miguel Ruiz
The Five Languages of Love: How to Express Heartfelt Commitment to Your Mate	Gary Chapman
The Invisible Touch: The Four Keys to Modern Marketing	Harry Beckwith
The HR Scorecard: Linking People, Strategy, and Performance	Mark A. Huselid, Dave Ulrich, Brian Becker

The Joy of Work	Scott Adams
The Leadership Challenge	James M. Kouzes & Barry Z. Posner
The Leadership Engine: How Winning Companies Build Leaders at Every Level	Noel M. Tichy
The Leadership Secrets of Colin Powell	Oren Harari
The Mastery of Love: A Practical Guide to the Art of Relationship	Don Miguel Ruiz
The Mind of the Soul: Responsible Choice	Gary Zukav & Linda Francis
The New Peoplemaking	Virginia Satir
The On Purpose Person: Making Your Life Make Sense	Kevin W. McCarthy
The Path of Action	Jack Schwarz
The Power of Full Engagement: Managing Energy, Not Time, Is the Key to High Performance, Health & Happiness	Jim Loer & Tony Schwartz
The Power of Now: A Guide to Spiritual Enlightenment	Eckhart Tolle
The Purpose-Driven Life	Rick Warren
The Seat of the Soul	Gary Zukov
The Rise of the Creative Class and How It's Transforming Work, Life, Community and Everyday Life	Richard L. Florida
The Servant: A Simple Story About the True Essence of Leadership	James C. Hunter
The Servant Leader: How to Build a Creative Team, Develop Great Morale, and Improve Bottom Line	James A. Autry
The Seven Habits of Highly Effective People	Stephen R. Covey

The Tipping Point: How Little Things Can Make a Big Difference	Malcolm Gladwell
The Travelers Gift	Andy Andrews
The War of Art: Winning the Inner Creative Battle	Steven Pressfield
The Way of Harmony: Walking the Inner Path to Balance, Happiness and Success	Jim Dreaver
The World's Most Powerful Leadership Principle: How to Become a Servant Leader	James C. Hunter
Thinkertoys: A Handbook of Business Creativity	Michael Michalko
Tuesdays With Morrie	Mitch Albom
Unstoppable: 45 Powerful Stories of Perseverance and Triumph From People Just Like You	Cynthia Kersey
Way of the Peaceful Warrior: A Book That Changes Lives	Dan Millman
Whale Done! The Power of Positive Relationships	Ken Blanchard
What Clients Love: A Field Guide to Growing Your Business	Harry Beckwith
What Should I Do With My Life?	Po Bronson
What You Think of Me is None of My Business	Terry Cole-Whittaker
When Things Fall Apart: Heart Advice for Difficult Times	Pema Chodron
Who Moved My Cheese? An Amazing Way to Deal With Change in Your Work and in Your Life	Spencer Johnson, M.D.
Women as Winners	Dorothy Jongeward & Scott Dru

Endnotes

1. Blanchard and Hodges, *Lead Like Jesus: Lessons from the Greatest Leadership Role Model of All Time.* W. Publishing Group, 2006.

2. Sanborn, Mark. *The Fred Factor.* Currency, 2004.

3. Munroe, Myles. *The Spirit of Leadership.* Whitaker House, 2005.

4. Konczal, Ed and Galvanek, Jeannette. *Simple Stories for Leadership Insight.* University Press of America, 2005.

5. "Human Resource Planning". The Human Resource Planning Society, (2004) Vol. 27, No. 1.

6. Goleman, Daniel. "What Makes a Leader". *Harvard Business Review.* 1998.

7. "Emotional Intelligence." Byron Stock & Associates, 1999.

8. Ibid.

9. Ibid

10. *HBR.* Nov./Dec., 1998.

11. "Developing Emotional Intelligence Skills". Byron Stock & Associates, 1999.

12. Ibid.

13. Michael Useem, Jerry Useem, and Paul Asel. *Upward Bound: Nine Original Accounts of How Business Leaders Reached Their Summits.* Crown Business, 2003.

14. Munroe.

15. Conger, J.A. "Charismatic and Transformational Leadership in Organizations: An Insider's

Perspective on These Developing Streams of Research." *Leadership Quarterly*, (1999) 10(2).

16. Goleman, D., Boyatzis, R., & McKee, A. *Primal Leadership*. Boston: Harvard Business School Press, 2002.

17. Collins, J. *Good to Great*. Harper Business: New York, 2001.

18. Barrett, Ann; Beeson, John. *Developing Business Leaders for 2010*. New York, NY : Conference Board, 2002.

19. Rudderman, Marion. *Standing at the Crossroads: Next Steps for High Achieving Women*. Jossey-Bass/Wiley, 2006.

20. Covey, Stephen R. *7 Habits of Highly Effective People*. Free Press, 2004.

21. Sykes, Ed. www.thesykesgroup. 2000.

22. Ibid.

23. Spears, Larry C. "Practicing Servant-Leadership" *Leader to Leader*. Fall 2004.

24. Ibid.

25. Ibid.

26. Cetron, Marvin J. and Davies, Owen. "Trends Now Shaping the Future". *The Futurist*, (2005) Vol 39.

27. Gary, Jay. www.jaygary.com. 2006.

28. Mintzberg, Henry. *Managers not MBAs: A Hard Look at the Soft Practice of Managing and Management Development*. Berrett-Koehler, 2005.

29. Slaughter, R. *The Foresight Principle*. Westport: Praeger.

30. Schwartz, P. *The Art of the Long View.* Doubleday. 1991.

31. Slaughter.

32. Ibid.

33. Ibid.

34. Schwartz.

35. Marsh, N., & McAllum, M. *Strategic foresight: the power of standing in the future.* Crown Content, 2002.

36. King, Jr., Martin Luther, quoted in *Great Quotes from Famous Leaders.* Unknown.

37. Collins, Jame C. andd Porras, Jerry I., *Built to Last: Successful Habits of Visionary Companies,* HarperBusiness, 1997.

38. Finzel. "Creating the Right Leadership Culture." Unkown.

39. Herb Baum, Tammy Kling, *The Transparent Leader: How to Build a Great Company through Straight Talk, Openness, and Accountability.* Collins, 2005.

40. Ibid.

41. Moss Kanter, Rosabeth. *Confidence: How winning streaks and losing streaks begin and end.* Three Rivers Press, 2004.

42. Hock, Dee. "The Art of Chaordic Leadership." *Leader to Leader.* Winter, 2000.

43. Goleman, Daniel. *Emotional Intelligence: Why It Can Matter More Than IQ.* Bantham, 1997.

44. Goleman, Daniel. "The Emotional Intelligence of Leaders," *Leader to Leader.* Fall, 1998.

45. *CEO Magazine.* Martin, 2003.

46. Bass, B.M. & Steidlmeier, P. "Ethics, Character, and Authentic Transformational Leadership Behavior." *Leadership Quarterly*, 10, 1999.

47. Ball, Jo. "Are You The Most Powerful Leader That You Can Be?" www.jogena.com.

48. Daily Quote 2002.

49. Author Unknown

50. Biro, Brian. *Beyond Success: The 15 Secrets of a Winning Life.* Perigee Trade; 2001.

51. Bennis, Warren, *Leader to Leader,* quoted in NetFax, 1997.

52. Goleman, Daniel. "Leading Resonant Teams". www.leadertoleader.org, 2002.

53. ibid

54. www.ccl.org.

55. Bennis, Warren "The Secrets of Great Groups" *Leader to Leader.* Winter, 1997.

56. Barker, *Future Edge.*

57. Van Deventer, Brian. *Beginning to Manage.* Vision Publishing, 2007.

58. Abraham Lincoln, quoted in *Great Quotes from Famous Leaders.* Unknown

59. Williams, Ken. *Ten Biblical Ways to Diffuse an Attack.* Wycliffe Bible Translators, 1996.

60. "What to Say When Two Members Won't Stop Fighting," *Practical Supervision,* December 1977.

61. Barker.

62. Gandossy, Robert and Verma, Nidhi. "Passing the Torch of Leadership". *Leader to Leader.* Spring, 2006.

☐

Printed in the United Kingdom
by Lightning Source UK Ltd.
130584UK00001B/217-222/P